PROJECT AIR FORCE

T0308270

Reducing Air Force Fighter Pilot Shortages

Albert A. Robbert, Anthony D. Rosello, Clarence R. Anderegg, John A. Ausink, James H. Bigelow, William W. Taylor, James Pita

Prepared for the United States Air Force

For more information on this publication, visit www.rand.org/t/RR1113

Library of Congress Cataloging-in-Publication Data is available for this publication.
ISBN: 978-0-8330-9173-4

Published by the RAND Corporation, Santa Monica, Calif.
© Copyright 2015 RAND Corporation
RAND® is a registered trademark.

Support RAND
Make a tax-deductible charitable contribution at
www.rand.org/giving/contribute

www.rand.org

Preface

The Air Force has faced a persistent challenge in that active-component fighter pilot requirements (particularly nonflying staff requirements) exceed its capacity to train and provide initial operational experience to a sufficient number of officers to fill these requirements. The objective of this report is to examine alternatives available to help close the resulting gaps. Since some solutions would rely on reserve-component resources, we also examined prevailing shortages of fighter pilots in the reserve components.

This research was sponsored by four elements of the U.S. Air Force: the Deputy Chief of Staff for Operations (AF/A3); the Deputy Chief of Staff for Manpower, Personnel and Services (AF/A1); the Commander, Air Force Reserve Command (AFRC/CC); and the Director, Air National Guard (NGB/CF). The research described in this report was conducted within the Manpower, Personnel, and Training Program of RAND Project AIR FORCE as part of a fiscal year 2014 study "Rated Requirements Assessment."

RAND Project AIR FORCE

RAND Project AIR FORCE (PAF), a division of the RAND Corporation, is the U.S. Air Force's federally funded research and development center for studies and analyses. PAF provides the Air Force with independent analyses of policy alternatives affecting the development, employment, combat readiness, and support of current and future air, space, and cyber forces. Research is conducted in four programs: Force Modernization and Employment; Manpower, Personnel, and Training; Resource Management; and Strategy and Doctrine.

Additional information about PAF is available on our website:
http://www.rand.org/paf

This report documents work originally shared with the U.S. Air Force on October 16, 2014. The draft report, issued on October 31, 2014, was reviewed by formal peer reviewers and U.S. Air Force subject-matter experts.

Contents

Figures and Tables

Figures

Tables

Summary

Although overall Air Force pilot manning is adequate, the Air Force faces a persistent shortage of fighter pilots. The expected magnitude of the shortfall in the active component (AC) is shown in Figure S.1. Similar shortages exist in the reserve components (RCs)—the Air National Guard (ANG) and Air Force Reserve Command (AFRC)—but with a difference. The AC prioritizes its manning such that shortages are primarily in headquarters staffs and other billets outside of operational squadrons, while RC shortages are primarily in ANG operational squadrons. The objective of this report is to examine alternatives available to help close the resulting shortages.

Figure S.1. Projected Shortfall in AC Fighter Pilots

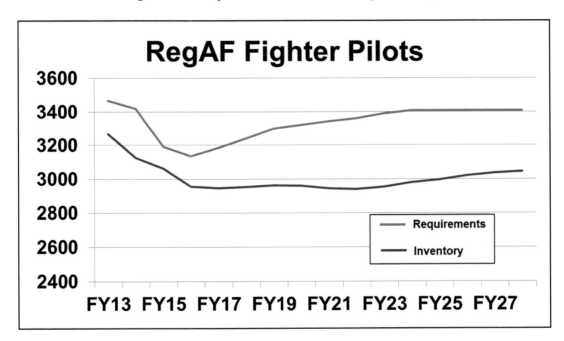

SOURCE: Headquarters United States Air Force (AF/A30-A), "Alt FY15 POM Fighter Impacts and Recommendations," 2013. Based on the alternate FY 2015 Program Objective Memorandum, including A-10, F-15C, and F-35 changes, large F-16 active associations, and some offset of AC requirements using Military Personnel Appropriation (MPA) man-days.

In the AC, the key elements that determine the size of the pilot inventory are the capacity to train new pilots (*production*), the capacity to introduce new pilots into operational units and give them enough flying time to turn them into experienced pilots (*absorption*), and the retention of experienced pilots that largely determines how many new pilots are required each year (*sustainment*). In the RCs, production and absorption are less critical because most of their sustainment needs are met by separating AC pilots who affiliate with RC units.

Production, absorption, and sustainment make up a dynamic system that is in balance only if long-run production and absorption capacities are greater than sustainment needs and if production does not exceed absorption capacity. During the past several decades, the Air Force has faced reductions in its fighter aircraft inventory that have caused its absorption capacity to fall below its sustainment needs, yielding persistent shortfalls, such as those depicted in Figure S.1. At times, production of new pilots was programmed at levels that would sustain required inventories but exceeded available absorption capacity. The result was broken units (due to too many inexperienced pilots in the units).

To eliminate its projected shortfalls, the Air Force may either increase the supply of pilots or reduce *certain types* of demands. Supply can be increased by increasing the number of operational aircraft that can be used to absorb new pilots (which also increases demand, but by a lesser amount than the associated increase in sustainable supply) or by increasing the absorption capacity of existing operational aircraft inventory. To help reduce shortfalls, reduction in demand must be taken in requirements outside of operational units, such as in headquarters staffs. That demand can be most readily reduced by substituting officers in career fields other than fighter pilot, civilians, or contractors (perhaps with a view toward hiring retired fighter pilots to fill those positions).

In our research for this project, we adopted a steady-state approach to evaluating various paths to a balanced system. A steady-state approach compares the long-run inventory impacts of any change in plans, programs, policies, and practices against a long-run requirement. It is a useful approach to identifying a *strategy* that will satisfy long-term needs while affording buffers large enough to accommodate year-to-year perturbations in production, absorption, or sustainment.

In identifying and evaluating paths toward a balanced system, we first sought to exploit any benefits possible by using aircraft inventories in the RCs. Alternatives are establishing more active associate units manned primarily by inexperienced pilots (to provide increased absorption opportunities), increasing use of RC pilots to meet AC requirements, and transferring units that exclusively require experienced pilots from the AC to the RCs. We found, however, that persistent shortages of fighter pilots in RC operational units seriously limit the potential for alternatives that would take additional pilots out of RC units. Of the alternatives mentioned here, only increased use of active associate units, which puts AC pilots in RC units and therefore can help to fill gaps in RC units, seems to have great potential.

A base case, approximating the status quo, and an alternative path whose feasibility we evaluated have the features shown in Table S.1. The alternative path assumes increased use of simulators, more first-assignment instructor pilots (FAIPs) going into fighter units, an optimistic retention outlook as measured by fighter-specific total active rated service (TARS), more active associate units, and limited use of reservists filling AC requirements. The path would yield a total inventory of 3,250 fighter pilots. Compared with an assumed long-run requirement for 3,450 AC fighter pilots, it would leave an expected shortfall of 200 experienced pilots.

Table S.1. Base Case and an Alternative Path Toward Balance

Feature	Base Case	Alternative Path
Fleet size	641 fighter aircraft in the AC. This is the long-run primary mission aircraft inventory (PMAI) in AC operational units after planned recapitalization of the fighter fleet.	Same
Required fighter flying to reach experienced level	Non-FAIPs – 500 hours, FAIPs – 300 hours	Same
Live flying	10 SCM with 1.4 hours average sortie duration	Same
Simulator credit toward experienced level	None	20 percent of required hours
Proportion of FAIPs in new pilot absorptions	12 percent	24 percent
Retention (fighter-specific TARS)	Non-FAIPS – 14 years, FAIPs - 11 years	Non-FAIPs – 16 years, FAIPs – 13 years
Annual active associate absorptions	Two each in four eight-pilot units and one in a four-pilot unit	Two each in four eight-pilot units and one each in 15 four-pilot units
Reservists filling AC requirements	None	10
Annual absorptions per squadron	5.4	7.0
Sustainable AC inventory	2,083	3,250

Variations on the path provide some insight on the strength of various factors. The remaining shortfall of 200 experienced pilots could be eliminated by increasing aircraft utilization rates. On the other hand, the gap would grow back to 400 if retention remains at current levels. We conclude from our analysis that alternatives to increase the available supply of fighter pilots have limited potential, and, based on discussions with Air Force aircrew managers, this potential may be much more limited than many decisionmakers realize. Accordingly, if balance is to be achieved, it will require reductions in demand.

Our analysis suggests that a reduction of 400 requirements (primarily by converting staff or other nonoperational positions from fighter pilot to other workforce types) would result in a relatively robust system. A useful way to allocate the conversions is to mirror the priorities in recent annual rated staff allocation plans (RSAPs). Withdrawing authorizations for active duty fighter pilots will motivate users of the positions to initiate the necessary shifts to other workforce types. However, recognizing that some such shifts (such as military-to-civilian conversions) require several complex programming steps, the Air Staff should seek ways to guarantee that initiated shifts are consummated.

A cautionary note is that this alternative path and its variations, with 7 to 7.5 new pilots absorbed annually in each squadron, would yield squadrons with 21 to 23 out of 30 line pilots on their first operational tour. This might provide insufficient opportunity for experienced pilots to serve second operational tours.

Yet another path toward balance would entail a shift in the mix of operational aircraft in the AC and RCs. Given the features in the alternative path in Table S.1, 11 additional 24-PMAI squadrons in the AC, with a corresponding decrease of 14 18-PMAI squadron in the RCs, would eliminate the 400-pilot gap left with that path. In addition to reducing or eliminating fighter pilot shortages in the AC, such a shift in the force mix would also reduce or eliminate fighter pilot shortages in the RCs. (Increased AC inventories would yield more separation of AC pilots, hence a larger pool available for affiliation with RC units and fewer units across which to spread the available affiliations.) There is a strong consensus among Air Force leaders against a shift in this direction and significant organizational and political obstacles that would need to be overcome, but prior research indicates that cost may not be a barrier. If more complete cost assessments confirm that varying force mixes are similar in cost, this path warrants consideration.

We conclude that various combinations of improved absorption, improved retention, increased AC force structure, and reduced requirements can be used to eliminate inventory shortfalls and create needed buffers in production and absorption processes. We do not advocate a policy of strictly limiting demand to the expected supply in every time period. To do so would make requirements, particularly staff requirements, more volatile than is necessary. However, once the system is rebalanced, it is possible that unfavorable trends in aircraft inventories, utilization rates, pilot retention, and other related factors could again make stated requirements unsustainable. The Air Force's interests will be best served by remaining alert to the possibility that unfavorable trends have become unalterable and, should that occur, again making the necessary adjustments to balance production, absorption, and sustainment.

Acknowledgments

This research underlying this report builds on an extended relationship between RAND Project AIR FORCE and the Air Force's aircrew management community. That community meets semi-annually under the auspices of the Air Force's Aircrew Management Executive Council, chaired by the Air Force Directorate of Operations Force Management, and has continually welcomed our engagement in their issues and challenges. During the period of this research, Colonel Douglas J. Nikolai and Mr. C.J. Ingram, of that office, were especially helpful in guiding our efforts. Our colleague Chuck Armentrout, who prior to retirement from the Air Force served in several key posts related to aircrew management, provided useful comments on the draft report. Critical review was provided by Ray Conley, director of the Manpower, Personnel, and Training Program within RAND Project AIR FORCE, and by our colleagues Bernard Rostker and Lawrence Hanser. The document benefited from careful editing by James Torr.

Abbreviations

AC	active component
ACA	aerospace control alert
ACC	Air Combat Command
AETC	Air Education and Training Command
AF/A1M	Air Force Directorate of Manpower, Organization, and Resources
AF/A1P	Air Force Directorate of Force Management Policy
AFGSC	Air Force Global Strike Command
AFI	Air Force Instruction
AFPC	Air Force Personnel Center
AFR	Air Force Reserve
AFRAMS	Air Force Rated Aircrew Management System [Model]
AFSC	Air Force specialty code
AGR	active Guard/reserve
ALO	air liaison officer
AMLO	air mobility liaison officer
ANG	Air National Guard
CSAF	Chief of Staff of the Air Force
FAIP	first-assignment instructor pilot
FTU	formal training unit
HAF	Headquarters Air Force
IP	instructor pilot
MAJCOM	major command
MPA	military personnel appropriation
MPES	Manpower Programming and Execution System
MTC	mission training center
O&M	operations and maintenance

OCO	overseas contingency operations
PAA	primary aircraft authorization
PMAI	primary mission aircraft inventory
POM	program objective memorandum
PPBE	planning, programming, budgeting, and execution [system]
PTAI	primary training aircraft inventory
RC	reserve component
RPA	reserve personnel appropriation
RSAP	rated staff allocation plan
SCM	sorties per crew per month
SOCOM	U.S. Special Operations Command
STRATCOM	U.S. Strategic Command
SUPT	specialized undergraduate pilot training
TARS	total active rated service
TFAM	Total Force Aircrew Management

1. Introduction

Although overall Air Force pilot manning is adequate, the Air Force faces a persistent shortage of fully qualified and experienced fighter pilots. It has faced this shortfall for most of the period since the post–Cold War drawdown of fighter aircraft force structure. The force structure drawdown created an imbalance—not enough fighter aircraft to provide training and experience to produce the total number of trained/experienced fighter pilots required to meet all operational and staff needs. This objective of this report is to examine alternatives available to help close the resulting shortages.

Figure 1.1 depicts the projected supply (inventory) and demand (requirements) of active-component (AC) Air Force fighter pilots. It follows the Air Force's canonical approach to depicting the available or anticipated supply of aviators (personnel inventory) and demand (manpower requirements). In the figure, expected fiscal-year-end requirements in the current and 20 future years are depicted as a red line; the corresponding inventory is depicted as a blue line.[1] Figure 1.1 shows that the fighter pilot shortage may approach 12 percent of forecast requirements in some years (but could be higher or lower because underlying assumptions, such as A-10 divestiture, are uncertain). In their simplest form, charts such as Figure 1.1 depict the best available expectation of the health of an aircrew inventory, either in the aggregate or in a specific component or type of aircraft.[2]

Various offices within the three Air Force total force components (the AC, Air Force Reserve Command [AFRC], and the Air National Guard [ANG]) have developed approaches to constructing red-line/blue-line charts. These approaches vary in their rigor and in their sources of information. To provide a more consistent approach, RAND Project AIR FORCE (PAF) has developed a comprehensive red-line/blue-line methodology for all aircrew types, rated communities, and components. The essentials of this methodology are described in Appendix B.

---

[1] Similar charts are generated for each aircrew type (pilot, combat systems officer, and various career enlisted aviator types), rated community (fighter; bomber; command, control, intelligence, surveillance, reconnaissance; combat search and rescue, mobility, and special operations), and component (AC, AFRC, ANG).

[2] Constructing projected red lines is largely a matter of deriving manpower requirements information from the Air Force planning, programing, budgeting, and execution (PPBE) system. In some cases, programming decisions are explicitly implemented as manpower requirements reflected in the Manpower Programming and Execution System (MPES). In other cases, analysts must estimate the requirements of expected changes not reflected in MPES. Constructing projected blue lines requires a modeling capability to "age" the current inventory by estimating the losses occurring in each future year. It also requires an estimate of new aircrew entering the inventory each year, based on either known training pipeline distributions or projected requirements.

Figure 1.1. Projected Shortfall in AC Fighter Pilots

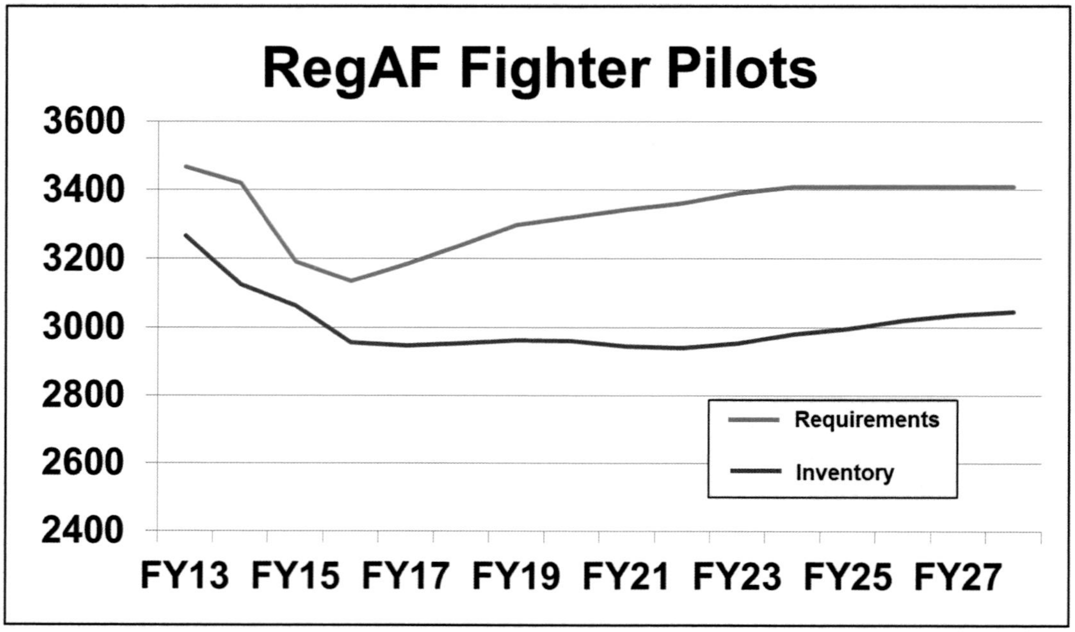

SOURCE: Headquarters United States Air Force (AF/A30-A), "Alt FY15 POM Fighter Impacts and Recommendations," 2013. Based on the alternate FY 2015 Program Objective Memorandum (POM), including A-10, F-15C, and F-35 changes, large F-16 active associations, and some offset of AC requirements using military personnel appropriation (MPA) man-days.

Another, nearer-term depiction of shortfalls is provided by the annual rated staff allocation plan (RSAP) developed by Air Force aircrew management staffs and approved by the Air Force Chief of Staff. This plan guides the distribution of available aircrew inventory to various using organizations by the Air Force Personnel Center (AFPC). A summary version of the FY 2014 RSAP is shown in Figure 1.2. The figure shows that, as of FY 2014, the Air Force was manning operational units with fighter pilots at 100 percent of authorizations and headquarters staffs at about 50 percent of authorizations.[3]

---

[3] The remaining positions were not all vacant, with many filled with other officers (often mobility pilots or air battle managers). For example, for FY 2014, Air Combat Command (ACC) had billets for 131 fighter pilots, 64 of which were filled with fighter pilots. However filling some of these positions with mobility pilots and air battle managers bought the overall manning for these positions up to 73 percent.

Figure 1.2. FY 2014 Rated Staff Allocation Plan (RSAP) Summary

Category	Organizations		Tot Req	Tgt	Tot Ent	Ftr Req	Tgt	Ftr Ent
Line Flying	Line Flying Units	Fly Students/Transients/PME	16126	100%	16111	446	98%	435
		Line CC Units/MPEP				1211	100%	1211
		FAIPs/IFF IPs/FTU IPs/ETSS				585	100%	585
		11F T-38 ALFA Tours				211	75%	158
		11F T-6 ALFA Tours				101	35%	35
		11F AGRS/CTS/WIC/57Wg				185	100%	185
		11F AFCENT AWC/TLP				5	80%	4
		11F RPA				66	30%	20
ALO/AMLO	ALO/AMLO (Rated req. adjusted for 13L growth)		224	100%	224	44	100%	44
OSD/JCS/ COCOMs	OSD; JCS; AFRICOM; CENTCOM; EUCOM; JFCOM; NATO; NORAD; NORTHCOM; PACOM; SOCOM; SOUTHCOM; STRATCOM; TRANSCOM		528	100%	528	84	51%	43
Test Flying	DCMA; ACC; AFMC; AFSOC; AMC; AFOTEC		596	97%	577	195	90%	176
Staff	SAF/HAF; ACC; AETC; AFGSC; AFSOC; AMC; PACAF; USAFE; AF Elements; Def Agencies; AFMC; AFRC; AFSC; AFSPC; ANG; AFDW; AFOTEC; AFISRA; AFSA; AFPC; USAFA; AU; IAS; ANG/AFRC Advisors		2407	97%	2330	353	51%	179
			19881	99%	19770	3486	88%	3075
NOTE: ~150 "surplus" ABMs fill many staff requirements								

SOURCE: Headquarters United States Air Force (AF/A3O-A briefing), "Rated Staff Allocation Plan (RSAP)", 2013.

Addressing Fighter Pilot Shortages

Efforts to reduce these persistent shortages have, at times, focused on increasing the production of new pilots to levels that would sustain the sum of operational and staff requirements. Those efforts, however, tended to ignore a critical intervening constraint—absorption of new fighter pilots in operational units. As discussed in Appendix D, which provides a historical perspective on efforts to address fighter pilot shortfalls, production in excess of absorption capacity results in unacceptable degradation of training and readiness in operational units. Basically, it results in spreading available flying hours too thinly across inexperienced pilots, slowing their development.

During the past five years, the Air Force has made a concerted effort to keep production and absorption in balance and to address overall pilot shortages through reductions in staff requirements or conversion of active duty fighter pilot positions to other workforce types, such as mobility pilots or civilian/contractor positions filled by retired or separated fighter pilots.[4] In 2009, for example, CORONA Top (one of the Air Force's quarterly senior leadership meetings) approved the recategorization of 837 rated billets to something other than rated (e.g., civilian,

---

[4] Readers may readily recognize the term *fighter* pilot. *Mobility* pilot may be less familiar. It refers to pilots operating tanker or airlift aircraft.

Guard or Reserve, nonrated Air Force specialty code [AFSC], career enlisted aviator), at a time when the overall rated shortfall exceeded 2,000 (Headquarters United States Air Force [AF/A1 and AF/A3/5], "Rated Staff Requirements IPT Implementation," 2009). In another example, at a Rated Summit (gathering of senior Air Force leaders to consider rated management issues) in 2011, agreement was reached to reduce another 710 pilot requirements (Headquarters United States Air Force [AF/A3O-AI], "Rated Summit Requirements Review," 2011).[5]

In principle, the Air Force Directorate of Operations Force Management (AF/A3O-A) exercises considerable authority over aircrew manpower authorizations. This office sets each major command's (MAJCOM's) maximum number of authorizations for pilots and other rated career fields, by aircrew position indicator (AFI 38-201, p. 65).[6] These policy provisions provide rated force managers much greater authority over details in rated manpower authorizations than is common in other functional areas.[7] In practice, however, Air Force decision processes tend to entail coordination and concurrence rather than unilateral direction to the MAJCOMs regarding rated force management issues. Thus, Air Staff aircrew managers sometimes allow imbalances between demand and supply to persist, notwithstanding their formal authority to constrain the demand.

By 2014, efforts on the demand side, along with developments on the supply side, such as overproduction of mobility pilots to offset fighter pilot shortfalls, had resulted in balance in the overall supply and demand of active duty pilots. Nonetheless, a shortage of fighter pilots has persisted in both the AC and the reserve components (RCs). Air Staff rated force managers saw little opportunity for consensus on further reductions in fighter pilot requirements and asked RAND Project AIR FORCE (PAF) to readdress the available alternatives.

Organization of the Report

In Chapter Two, we describe the dynamics of managing the fighter pilot inventory and list alternatives available to reduce shortages. In Chapter Three, we discuss alternatives available to reduce fighter pilot shortfalls by increasing supply. In Chapter Four, we discuss alternatives to reduce demand. In Chapter Five, we recommend paths toward a balanced system that eliminates persistent shortages. Appendixes provide details regarding an absorption model used in our analysis, documentation of a total force aircrew inventory model we provided to the Air Staff as part of the project underlying this report, an assessment of RC fighter pilot shortages, an

---

[5] This agreement called for eliminating 45 fighter pilot requirements in remotely piloted aircraft (RPAs), 200 generalist pilot staff positions, 140 fighter T-6 instructor pilot and first assignment instructor pilot (FAIP) positions, and 60 T-38 instructor pilot positions; converting 65 air liaison officer and 200 staff and test billets.

[6] Aircrew position indicators identify 18 categories of aircrew positions, differentiating on characteristics such as enlisted versus officer, pilot versus navigator, and staff versus operational.

[7] In other functional areas, MAJCOMs must adhere to overall allocations of manpower requirements, but Air Staff functional managers do not have the authority to limit the number of requirements established by the MAJCOMs *in specific career fields.*

assessment of the impact of past fighter pilot force structure reductions along with a summary of key management decisions, and a history of past fighter pilot staff reductions.

2. Aircrew Management Dynamics

In this chapter, we describe the essential elements of a dynamic aircrew management system and then outline how changes in the system can be introduced to reduce shortages. These changes will entail either an increase in supply or a decrease in demand.

Fundamental Elements

In the AC, the key elements that determine the size of the pilot inventory are the capacity to train new pilots (*production*), the capacity to introduce new pilots into operational units and give them enough flying time to turn them into experienced pilots (*absorption*), and the loss of experienced pilots that determines how many new pilots are required each year (*sustainment*).[1] Figure 2.1 illustrates the ideal relationship among these three elements of the pilot management system. The system is in balance when inventories can be sustained within available production and absorption capacities. Production capacity has an optimum level: If too low, sustainment requirements are not met; if too high, resources are unnecessarily expended on the training pipeline. Absorption capacity, on the other hand, is largely a by-product of operational capacity and thus does not have an optimal upper bound.

Figure 2.1. Fundamental Elements of Pilot Management

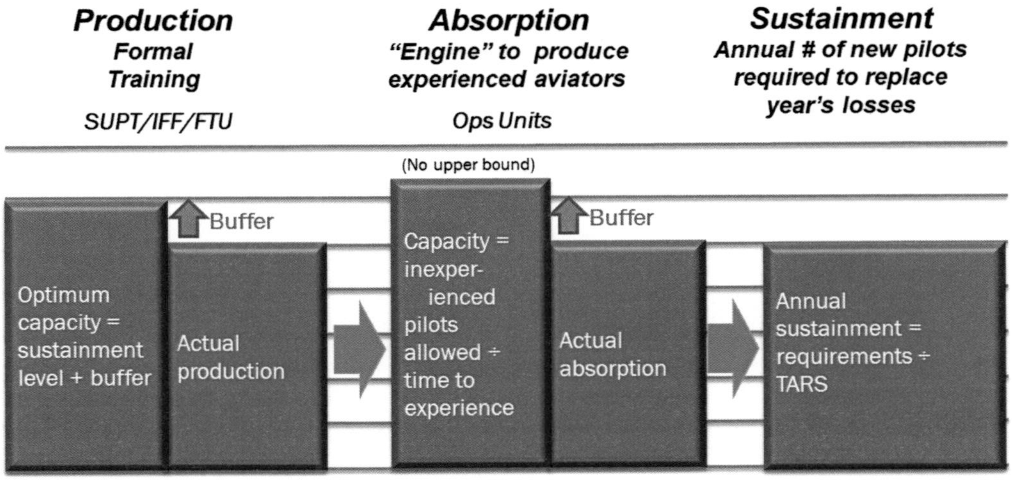

NOTES: SUPT = specialized undergraduate pilot training, IFF = introduction to fighter fundamentals, FTU = formal training unit, TARS = total active rated service.

---

[1] In the RCs, production and absorption play lesser roles, the major variables being the number of separating AC pilots and their propensity to affiliate with reserve units.

Training Production

The training pipeline for new pilots includes SUPT, which has separate fighter/bomber and airlift/tanker tracks. After graduation, pilots typically report to an FTU to become basically qualified in a specific aircraft mission-design series (MDS), preceded, in the case of fighter pilots, by an IFF course. Flying training pipelines require considerable resources, including aircraft, instructor pilots (IPs), maintenance workforces, spares, fuel, and munitions. Since these are expensive resources, excess training capacity should be avoided. However, as discussed below, the optimum training capacity includes a buffer to accommodate perturbations in absorption and sustainment requirements.

Absorption

Absorption capacity is derived from the need to maintain a balance between experienced and inexperienced pilots in a unit. Air Force policy (see Volume I of each of the AFI 11-2 series of publications for various aircraft types) defines flying-hour thresholds at which pilots are considered *experienced* and defines the conditions under which inexperienced and experienced pilots are permitted to fly. In many cases, inexperienced pilots must fly with experienced flight leaders. New fighter pilots coming directly out of SUPT and IFF require 500 flying hours to become designated as experienced. In certain cases, up to 100 of those hours can be credited in advanced simulators.

Absorption capacity is actually a prudent limitation rather than an absolute constraint. It can be exceeded—referred to as *overabsorption*—but doing so causes training and readiness problems. If the proportion of inexperienced pilots is too high, their opportunities to fly (since they generally must be accompanied by an experienced pilot) decline, which can result in unacceptably slow progression to the experienced threshold and unfavorable readiness to execute the unit's documented missions.[2] Taylor et al. (2002) demonstrated that these conditions begin to appear when the proportion of experienced pilots in a squadron falls below 60 percent. Subsequently, the Air Force adopted an objective of keeping the experienced level at or above 55 percent in its operational squadrons.[3] See Appendix D for a more detailed account of these considerations.

Annual absorption capacity can be calculated as the number of inexperienced pilots allowed in the unit divided by the average time in years required to become experienced. Time to become

---

[2] These conditions were notably observed in the A-10 fighter wing at Pope Air Force Base in 2000, giving rise to the term "Pope syndrome" to indicate the impacts of too many inexperienced pilots in a unit.

[3] The Air Force designates pilots by aircrew position indicator (API) code. The line pilots are designated as API-1 pilots, while pilots who fly in supervisory or staff positions at wing level or below are designated API-6 pilots. The 55 percent proportion applies to pilots in API 1 positions and was set as a goal by a 1999 Four-Star Summit (Taylor et al., 2000, p. xiv). Similar, though less demanding, requirements exist in mobility units.

experienced is, of course, a function of the available flying hours.[4] Like training capacity, absorption capacity should include a buffer to accommodate perturbations in sustainment requirements. However, unlike training capacity, there is no compelling reason to limit absorption capacity. The resources that produce absorption capacity are the same resources used to provide operational capability. Having slack absorption capacity simply means that units are operating with more than the minimum proportion of experienced pilots (as is common in RC units).

Pilot positions can be divided into two categories: *absorbing* and *nonabsorbing*. Absorbing positions are in operational units to which inexperienced pilots can be assigned.[5] An increase in absorbing positions allows an increase in total pilot inventory. Nonabsorbing positions are nonflying staff positions, or positions in flying units that use only experienced pilots (such as FTU, aggressor units where experienced pilots play the role of enemy pilots, or test units), or other types of duties that call for experienced pilots (such as air liaison officer [ALO] positions with the Army).

Sustainment

The final element in determining a pilot inventory is sustainment, which varies primarily as a function of requirements and retention. Pilots exit the AC inventory by separating or retiring from the Air Force, being promoted to colonel, death, or grounding. The sustainment level required is simply the number of new pilots required each year to replace pilots exiting the inventory.

A useful summary measure of retention behavior is TARS, which is the average number of years of service between SUPT graduation and exiting the fighter pilot inventory.[6] The required sustainment level can thus be estimated by dividing the inventory requirement by the appropriate TARS value.[7] Equilibrium conditions for the system require the number of new pilots entering

---

[4] Flying hours are a key factor in programming, budgeting, and execution of the resources required for aircraft operations. Flying hours generated by a unit are the product of the total number of primary mission aircraft inventory (PMAI) available and their utilization rates, consisting of the average number of sorties flown per PMAI per month and the average sortie duration.

[5] In its aircrew management documentation, the Air Force uses the terms *absorbable* and *nonabsorbable*. AFI 11-412 (2009, p. 63) defines an *absorbable unit* as "a flying unit that accepts inexperienced aircrew members into its crew force." The terms *absorbable* and *nonabsorbable* are used throughout AFI 11-412 in reference to units, aircraft, and positions. Rather than follow this convention, which literally indicates that the referenced units are or are not capable of being absorbed, we use terms indicating that the referenced units are or are not capable of doing the absorbing.

[6] The fighter pilot inventory is composed of pilots in the grade of O-5 and below, because colonels and above are managed separately from the normal aircrew management system,

[7] For example, if the Air Force had a requirement for 3,400 fighter pilots, the expected TARS of 14 years would mean that 3,400/14 = 243 fighter pilots would need to be produced each year. See Taylor, Bigelow, and Ausink (2009) and the references therein for more information on experience levels, API codes, TARS data, and pertinent formulas.

the operational fighter units each year (i.e., the production) to be equal to or less than the absorption capacity of those units and equal to the number of pilots lost from the fighter pilot inventory during the year (i.e., the required sustainment).

The Air Force uses historical data to calculate observed TARS. Pilots incur an active duty service commitment of ten years upon graduation from SUPT. Since many pilots will remain beyond their initial commitment, expected TARS for any current or future pilot population is greater than ten years. Computed from recent retention rates, it is about 14 years for AC fighter pilots. Although the term *active service* does not fit the RC context, a similar measure of aviation service applies to the RCs. Another indicator of retention behavior is the proportion of pilots completing their active duty service commitments who accept a pilot retention bonus. Over the past several decades, acceptance rates generally have ranged from 30 to 40 percent during periods of high airline hiring and from 60 to 70 percent during periods of low airline hiring. Anticipated acceptance rates can be used to estimate expected TARS.

Guard and Reserve units are sustained principally by affiliating prior-service pilots as they separate from the AC. However, RC units also augment their manning with pilots with no prior service who are commissioned and trained for their specific units.

Buffers

The production and absorption processes are dynamic queuing systems that become *saturated* when operated consistently at or near 100 percent of capacity. External factors will generate perturbations within the system that require adjustments to restore balance. The ability to make these adjustments requires *buffers*. Saturated systems are inherently unstable and become very difficult to adjust and return to equilibrium conditions. A 15–20 percent buffer is suggested in the research literature to ensure that essential adjustments can be made (Kleinrock, 1975).[8] The required buffers account for the differences between production or absorption capacities and required production or absorption levels in Figure 2.1.

Modeling Absorption Capacity

Although production capacity has at times been the binding constraint that causes pilot shortfalls, absorption capacity historically has been the problem. Training capacity can be kept at an acceptable level *relative to absorption capacity* by rebalancing *available* resources (aircraft, flying hours, pilots) between training and operational roles. However, resource constraints may and often have prevented the fighter fleet from absorbing enough pilots to sustain the required total inventory of pilots. We thus made absorption capacity a central focus in our analysis of inventory shortfalls. For this focus, we needed to produce estimates of how specific absorption factors would affect pilot inventories.

---

[8] Unpublished discussions include Wikipedia (2014), Myers (undated), and Stallings (undated).

Appendix A provides a detailed description of a steady-state model we created to estimate fighter absorption capacities. The elements of the model are depicted in Figure 2.2. The model uses information about the aircraft, simulator, and aircrew resources at a squadron level to determine the absorption capacity of a unit. It then uses the calculated per-aircraft absorption capacity, fleet size, and other information to determine the size of the total pilot inventory that can be sustained by the fleet.

Figure 2.2. Elements of a Steady-State Fighter Absorption Model

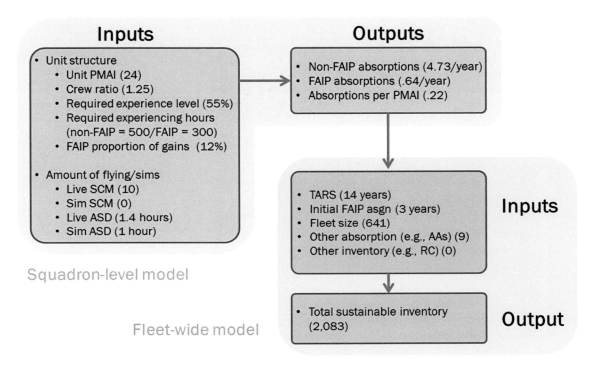

NOTES: SCM = sorties per crew per month, ASD = average sortie duration, AAs = active associate units. Figures in parentheses indicate base case values used in computations in Appendix A.

Addressing the Imbalances

With a ten-year active duty service commitment and with inexperienced pilots requiring roughly three years in an operational unit to be considered an "experienced" pilot, operational units will always be able to sustain more than their own requirement for a 55 percent experienced level.[9] However, to meet total pilot needs, absorbing positions must sustain total pilot inventories large enough to meet the sum of absorbing and nonabsorbing positions. Hence, many of the shortfall-

---

[9] If all pilots were retained for no more than the ten-year active duty service commitment, and allowing six months for IFF and FTU training after SUPT graduation, pilots would provide three years of inexperienced service and 6.5 years of experienced service. In a steady state, the experience level would be 68 percent (6.5 years/9.5 years).

reducing alternatives described below will entail either increases in absorbing positions or decreases in nonabsorbing positions.

Increasing Supply

Alternatives to increase the total steady-state inventory of AC fighter pilots depend on whether training production or absorption is the binding constraint. If training production is the binding constraint, inventory can be increased by shifting resources from operational to training purposes so that production capacity equals absorption capacity plus a suitable buffer. If absorption is the binding constraint, the following alternatives apply:

- Increase absorbing positions.

  - Increase operational force structure.
  - Shift resources from training to operational purposes.

- Increase absorption in available aircraft inventory.

  - Increase active associations (leveraging available aircraft and high experience levels in the RCs to support increased AC absorption).[10]
  - Shift force structure from the RCs to the AC, since the AC has greater capacity to absorb inexperienced pilots.
  - Reduce time-to-experience (e.g., increase simulator availability and aircraft utilization rates).
  - Reduce the flying-hour threshold for becoming "experienced."
  - Optimize use of FAIPs.[11]

- Increase pilot retention (but with due consideration for RC pilot inventory impacts).
- Increase the number of RC pilots serving in AC positions (using MPA man-days or limited-period recall to active duty).

Reducing Demand

Alternatives to reduce demand, focusing on nonabsorbing requirements, include the following:

- Convert AC nonabsorbing fighter pilot positions to other than AC fighter pilot positions (e.g., civilian, contractor, non–fighter pilot or nonpilot officer, career enlisted aviator, active Guard/reserve [AGR]).
- Transfer nonabsorbing positions from the AC to the RCs.
- Convert nonabsorbing positions to absorbing positions.
- Eliminate positions.

---

[10] *Active associations* are arrangements in which a small cell of AC pilots and maintainers are collocated with an RC unit and operate using the RC unit's aircraft. This is in contrast to classical associations, in which RC units (generally wings) are collocated with an AC wing and operate its aircraft.

[11] FAIPs are pilots whose first assignment following SUPT was as an SUPT instructor pilot.

Alternatives to increase supply are discussed in the following chapter. Alternatives to reduce demand are discussed in Chapter Four.

3. Increasing Supply

As outlined in the previous chapter, increasing supply generally depends on increases in new-pilot training production, absorption, and/or retention but can also be achieved through increased use of RC resources to meet AC requirements. In this chapter, we reiterate the importance of keeping production, absorption, and sustainment balanced, then discuss and evaluate approaches for increasing supply.

Training Production

The practical relationships between training capacity, absorption capacity, and sustainment are in some ways more complex than the relationships depicted in Figure 2.1. First, consider a case, typical for the fighter community, in which absorption capacity is below the required sustainment level. If training capacity exceeds this absorption capacity plus an appropriately sized buffer, the training pipeline claims resources that could otherwise be used to increase absorption (e.g., training aircraft and flying hours that could otherwise be transferred to operational units) or to fill nonabsorbing positions (e.g., instructor pilots who could otherwise serve in rated staff positions). Further, if this training capacity were used to actually produce above absorption levels, the result would be the deteriorated environments in operational units associated with overabsorption. Thus, when absorption capacity is practically limited to less than sustainment, training capacity should be no greater than absorption capacity plus a suitable buffer, and actual training production should be closely aligned with absorption capacity.

If absorption capacity were greater than the required sustainment level (an unexpected case in the fighter community, but possible in other rated communities), some absorption capacity would remain unused, and therefore the economical level of training capacity would be less than absorption capacity. In that case, training capacity should be at the level of sustainment plus a suitable buffer and actual training production should be closely aligned with sustainment requirements.

As discussed above, a shift of resources from operational to training units may be required to bring the pilot management system closer to equilibrium. However, this might require an unacceptable reduction in available operational force structure. Under these circumstances, decisionmakers must weigh trade-offs between operational force structure and total pilot inventory. Addressing those trade-offs is beyond the scope of our current research.

15

Absorption

Absorption can be increased by increasing the number of absorbing positions or by increasing the absorption capacity of existing force structure.

Increasing Absorbing Positions

The most straightforward approach to increasing fighter absorption is to increase the number of fighter pilot positions in AC units that can accept inexperienced pilots. This can be achieved by increasing total fleet size, shifting force structure from test or training to operational units, shifting force structure from the RCs to the AC, or increasing crew ratios in operational units. Each of these alternatives, of course, involves costs and competing considerations that must be weighed against the gain in absorption capacity. Because of the high costs involved, feasibility is limited.

Increasing Absorption Capacity in Existing Force Structure

One feasible approach to increasing the absorption capacity of existing force structure, partially implemented, is increasing the number and size of active associate cells in RC fighter units. This approach uses RC resources—both aircraft and experienced pilots—to increase the absorbing positions available for inexperienced AC pilots. The prevailing models for these cells, designed specifically to provide increased absorption capacity, are four AC pilots (one experienced, three inexperienced) or eight pilots (one experienced, seven inexperienced).[1] Given the very high experience levels in RC flying units, there is considerable capacity in terms of experienced aircrew members to host these active associate cells. These cells have the potential added benefit of helping to break down cultural barriers between the AC and the RCs. Additionally, by filling out part of the required crew ratio associated with their host units' aircraft, they reduce or eliminate persistent pilot shortages in RC fighter units (see Appendix C for a discussion of these shortages).

We have estimated (see footnote 19) that each four-pilot associate cell could support the absorption of a little over one new active pilot per year and that each eight-pilot cell could support over two per year. There are currently five active associate cells, plus another potential 14 or more, depending on force structure decisions not yet finalized as of the end of FY 2014.

---

[1] These active associate cells absorb more pilots than would be possible if the aircraft used by the associate cell were moved to the AC. Assume that AC units should be 45 percent inexperienced, time to reach an experienced level is 2.7 years (see Appendix A), and crew ratio is 1.25. A 24-PMAI AC unit thus has a crew force of 30 pilots, of whom 13.5 can be inexperienced, and an absorption capacity of 13.5/2.7 = 5 per year, or 0.21 absorptions per cockpit per year. Alternatively, an active associate cell with one experienced and three inexperienced pilots, at a crew ratio of 1.25, constructively occupies 3.2 RC cockpits. Absorption capacity in these active associate cells is 3/2.7 = 1.1 absorptions per year, or 0.35 absorptions per cockpit per year. In practice, rotations out of associate units might occur after three years rather than 2.7 years, reducing absorption capacity for the four-pilot cell to 1 per year, or 0.31 absorptions per cockpit per year. Absorption capacity for an active associate cell at 0.31/cockpit/year is greater than the 0.21/cockpit/year in the AC. A similar favorable absorption outcome exists for eight-pilot active associate cells.

Four existing associations are eight-pilot cells embedded in 24-PAA (primary aircraft authorization) squadrons (three in AFRC, one in the ANG). The remaining extant association and all anticipated new associations are expected to eventually be four-pilot cell, although some may be initially implemented at a smaller scale (Headquarters United States Air Force [AF/A30-A], "CAF Active Association [AA] Update and Vector Check," 2014).

As indicated in the absorption modeling described in Appendix A, absorption capacity is increased when the time required to "age" new pilots—that is, give them enough flying hours to become experienced—is reduced. The current experience requirement for pilots with no previous weapon system qualification is 500 flying hours, of which 20 percent may be accumulated in simulator rather than live missions.[2] The time required to reach 500 hours (generally under three years at typical aircraft utilization rates in fighter units) can be reduced if resources required to increase flying hours, and hence aircraft utilization rates, can be made available. Additionally, holding flying hours constant, a unit with access to simulators that qualify as a substitute for live flying can reduce time to experience. Unfortunately, simulators of the prescribed quality are not available to all units.

It is also possible to increase absorption by simply reducing the 500-hour threshold required to reach an experienced level. Evaluating the safety and readiness implications of this change is beyond the scope of our current research, so we have not further evaluated this option.

Another avenue for increasing absorption capacity is to increase the proportion of FAIPs among inexperienced pilots flowing into the fighter pipeline. FAIPs reach an experienced level with 300 fighter hours rather than the 500 hours required of non-FAIPs. Holding total flying hours and the number of inexperienced pilots in a squadron constant, more new pilots per year can be absorbed as the FAIP proportion increases (see illustrative calculations in Appendix A). The illustrations also confirm that, notwithstanding reduced fighter-specific TARS,[3] increased FAIP input to fighter units will also increase expected total fighter pilot inventories. At the margin, doubling the proportion of FAIPs among inexperienced pilots allocated to AC fighter squadrons, from a recent level of 12 to 24 percent, would increase absorption capacity by 6 percent, resulting in a steady-state increase of 3 percent in the total AC fighter pilot inventory.[4]

The primary constraint on increasing FAIP absorption in fighter units is the composition of the Air Education and Training Command (AETC) instructor pilot workforce. AETC aircrew managers have indicated that some minimum proportion of non-FAIPs is needed to develop

---

[2] See AFI 11-2 documentation for each major design series.

[3] For FAIPs, fighter-specific TARS is the expected TARS for fighter pilots minus the time spent on their FAIP tour.

[4] There are limits to this approach. In the steady state, the total number of pilots entering a unit each year is constant. Increasing the FAIP ratio allows the unit to accept more inexperienced pilots each year, which decreases the number of available positions for *experienced* pilots who are ready to enter the unit for a second tour. This could have an impact on career development. FAIP increases also affect the instructor mix in SUPT units, with potentially adverse effects. As with other elements of the fighter pilot production system, the potential secondary effects of adjusting the FAIP ratio must be carefully considered.

instructor pilots for supervisory positions and other related needs. They indicate that the current proportion of FAIPs is at the maximum proportion consistent with these needs. Accordingly, sending more FAIPs to fighter units would have to come at the expense of sending fewer FAIPs to mobility and special operations forces (SOF) units. Since absorption constraints are less binding in mobility and SOF units, such a shift toward more fighter FAIPs should be considered.

Retention

At a fundamental level, the expected size of a rated AC inventory equals annual absorption multiplied by TARS. TARS is a function of retention, which in turn, for pilots, is largely a function of the rate at which pilots completing their initial active duty service commitment for pilot training choose to accept aviation continuation pay (ACP)—the so-called *take rate*. The Air Force generally seeks to maximize fighter pilot retention by using ACP as aggressively as possible and by advocating increases in statutory limits on ACP. In the past, the Air Force has also increased retention by lengthening, in several steps, the active duty service commitment for pilot training, currently at ten years.

TARS can be calculated from observed attrition of pilots in any single year, or from attrition averaged over multiple years.[5] Figure 3.1 shows a series of TARS calculations—some single-year and some multiyear. The figure shows that, over the past several decades, TARS has generally ranged between 12 and 18 years.

---

[5] A pending Air Force publication defines TARS and its calculation as follows:

> The number of years an officer serves in the rated force, from award of wings to separation, promotion to colonel, grounding, or retirement. TARS is computed by summing 2 through 28 years of [cumulative continuation rates]. TARS is one of the factors used in making inventory (Blue Line) projections. It can also be used to make simplified inventory projections. Two points to keep in mind are: 1) the TARS calculation is based on a projected steady state environment; and, 2) when any variable is changed that affects retention, TARS also changes.

$$TARS = \sum_{i=2}^{28} CCR_i$$

where i = years of rated service, CCR = cumulative continuation rate.

Figure 3.1. Historic TARS Values for AC Fighter Pilots

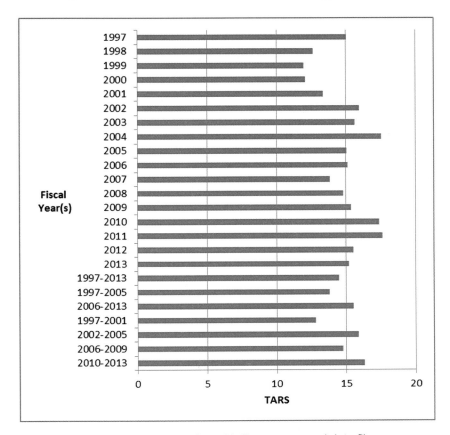

NOTE: TARS derived by authors from Air Force personnel data files.

Unfortunately, since affiliation of separating AC pilots is the primary source of RC accessions, increased AC retention decreases the flow of experienced pilots to the RCs. To account for fewer affiliations of separating AC pilots, the RCs must recruit and develop more of its own pilots, at considerable expense. As indicated in Appendix D, the RCs have also had difficulty filling their allocated SUPT quotas. Thus, AC retention initiatives need to be evaluated in a total-force context to determine the level that best meets the needs of all components.

Using RC Resources to Meet AC Requirements

A final alternative for increasing supply is to use RC pilots more liberally to fill AC positions that call for experienced pilots, particularly headquarters staff positions. Three mechanisms can be used for this purpose. A short-term approach is voluntary activation using MPA man-days. A longer-term approach is a voluntary recall to active duty (usually for a limited period of three years or less). The most permanent approach is to convert AC positions to full-time AGR positions.

19

In spite of programming and statutory impediments (see Robbert et al., 2014), all of these approaches are currently in use to some extent. MAJCOMs are using MPA man-days to fill some rated staff gaps. Impediments in this case include a management process that ties man-days to needs that can be programmed in advance rather than emerging needs and the difficulty, in many cases, of finding funds to cover the travel and per diem expenses of individuals whose pay and allowances are provided by man-day funding (Headquarters United States Air Force [MA to CSAF], "CSAF [Chief of Staff of the Air Force] Vector Check on ARC Requirements Management Process Improvement Initiative," 2014). Voluntary recalls to active duty occur periodically. A voluntary recall of RC pilots to active duty brought back about 400 pilots in 2009, and some are still on active duty. On a limited scale, AGR positions currently can be found in headquarters staffs. However, there is a statutory obligation to focus the AGRs' duties on reserve matters.

In addition to helping offset AC pilot shortages, having RC pilots serving on headquarters staffs has the potential to be a useful measure in itself: RC pilots can strengthen the RC voice on staffs that increasingly manage and employ both AC and RC assets, and joint and service headquarters staff experience better prepares RC pilots to fill senior leadership positions.

Unfortunately, a major impediment to this approach is the prevailing shortage of pilots in many RC fighter units (see Appendix C). Another impediment, observed by the authors at periodic Air Force forums focusing on aircrew management, is low awareness of opportunities to use these approaches among functional managers, assignment teams, commanders, and potential applicants.

4. Reducing Demand

To be beneficial in reducing fighter pilot shortfalls, reductions in demand must occur in either noncockpit positions or in nonabsorbing cockpit positions (e.g., test pilot positions). As described in Chapter Two, while RC cockpits make a contribution, absorbing cockpits in the AC are the engine that generates most pilot inventory. Reducing absorbing cockpits yields an immediate reduction in fighter pilot requirements; the red-line reduction in FYs 2015 and 2016, as shown in Figure 1.1, is just such a reduction—an impact of planned (although heretofore unrealized) A-10 divestitures. But the long-run impact of a reduction in absorbing fighter pilot requirements is an even greater reduction in pilot inventory, caused by loss of absorption capacity, contributing to, rather than mitigating, inventory shortfalls.

Noncockpit positions include three of the five categories shown in Figure 1.2 (the FY 2014 RSAP)—air and air mobility liaison officer positions (ALOs and AMLOs); staff positions within the Officer of the Secretary of Defense, Joint Staff, or combatant commander staffs; and other staff positions. In FY 2014, these three categories totaled 44, 84, and 353 requirements, respectively. For completeness, the expected fill of *institutional* positions by fighter pilots should also be recognized as a requirement.[1] These have been estimated at about 150. Thus, total noncockpit requirements were 631 in FY 2014.

Nonabsorbing cockpit requirements include most of the flying unit categories below the first two lines shown in Figure 1.2 (students/transients/professional military education and line combat-coded units), These totaled 1,155 positions in FY 2014.

Past Reductions

Over the past decade, the size of the Air Force, the number of fighter aircraft, and the number of fighter pilots have decreased. The number of fighter pilot requirements outside of line flying units (staff, test, and ALO/AMLO billets), representing most nonabsorbing fighter pilot requirements, has also decreased. Air Staff aircrew managers have told us that they advocated further cuts in staff billets in order to balance requirements with available inventory, but encountered significant push-back from the organizations that would have been affected and ultimately decided against further cuts, apparently with the hope that currently vacant positions might be filled at some point in the future. Additional information regarding past reductions can be found in Appendix F.

---

[1] *Institutional* positions are those that can be filled by officers from any career field. They include positions such as AFSC 97E (executive officer positions above the wing level, Pol-Mil Affairs Strategist, Regional Affairs Strategist, and Reserve Officers' Training Corps [ROTC] detachment commanders).

Even though the nonabsorbing billets have decreased, the Air Force still is unable to fill all of these positions. As indicated in Figure 1.2, the Air Force in FY 2014 planned to man its operational flying units at 100 percent while leaving staff positions filled at around 50 percent. Staff positions that cannot be filled by fighter pilots are often filled with other types of rated officers—an imperfect match of human capital to requirements.

Further Reductions

Options to reduce requirements, listed in Chapter Two, include converting AC nonabsorbing fighter pilot requirements to other than AC fighter pilot (civilian, contractor, non–fighter pilot or nonpilot officer, career enlisted aviator, AGR), transferring nonabsorbing requirements from the AC to the RC, converting nonabsorbing requirements to absorbing requirements, and eliminating nonabsorbing requirements. We will discuss each of these in turn.

Converting Fighter Pilot Requirements to Other Workforce Types

Staff requirements are the category most amenable to converting fighter pilot requirements to other workforce types, such as different officer career fields or civilian or contractor positions to be filled by separated or retired officers with fighter experience. Many positions with requirements for rated expertise in the Air Staff or the MAJCOMs are currently filled by civilians or contractors with prior rated experience, typically military retirees. Additionally, in past years, mobility pilots were purposely overproduced in order to maintain total pilot production numbers during periods when fighter pilot absorption or production constraints precluded producing the number of fighter pilots required to sustain that inventory. Some of these mobility pilots eventually were used to help fill fighter pilot shortfalls in staff positions.[2] While some staff positions may require current operational experience, many more that are currently tagged as fighter pilot requirements (and manned at 50 percent) might be effectively filled by retired fighter pilots or by non–fighter pilots—arguably more effectively than if left vacant.

The most straightforward shift to another workforce type is changing a manpower authorization from AFSC 11F (fighter pilot) to some other AFSC or career field, such as another pilot AFSC, 12F (fighter combat systems officer) or other combat systems officer AFSCs, 18x (remotely piloted aircraft pilot), 13B (air battle manager), or any other AFSC. A less straightforward approach, but one which may provide a better match of specific experience to requirements, is conversion of a military position to a civilian or contractor position, with a view toward filling the position with a separated or retired fighter pilot.

---

[2] Absorption of mobility pilots is generally not a problem when overseas contingency operations (OCOs) are in progress. The hours required for OCO support are typically additive and funded by the Transportation Working Capital Fund (TWCF) rather than by Air Force operations and maintenance funds. In many circumstances, these additional hours can contribute to qualifying, experiencing, and absorbing new pilots.

Reluctance to convert such positions to other available workforce categories may be attributable to a hope that supply might eventually match demand or to the difficulty and uncertainty of converting military to civilian positions. Giving up a military position to gain a civilian or contractor position requires several steps on the part of manpower, programming, and financial managers at the Air Staff and in the organizations in which the positions are established, with success not guaranteed. Because of these disincentives, conversions in the numbers required to eliminate fighter pilot shortfalls cannot be expected to occur at a useful scale if left to the initiative of the offices where the current requirements exist. Successful conversion at a useful scale will require centrally managed efforts and strong oversight. Through its monitoring and control of aircrew manpower authorizations (AFI 38-201, p. 77), the Air Force Directorate of Operations has the authority to motivate the required conversions (see discussion of this authority in Chapter One), but would require assistance from programming, financial management, and manpower management staffs to ensure that shifts from military to civilian or contractor positions are fully consummated.

Transferring Requirements from the AC to the RC

Some functions that were previously viewed as AC functions are now established missions within the RCs. Examples include the aerospace control alert (ACA) mission and certain FTU missions. Other fighter-oriented, nonabsorbing missions that might usefully be transferred to the RCs include aggressor and adversary air missions.

The principal impediment to transferring additional missions to the RCs is the limited supply of fighter pilots available to the RCs. Using recent data (AC separations from FYs1996 through 2007, ANG and AFRC affiliations from FY 1996 through 2013), PAF determined that 74 percent of separating AC pilots with between nine and 16 years of service affiliated with an ANG or AFRC unit within six years of separating. This very high rate of affiliation may be difficult to elevate. Additionally, because of the lengthy training pipeline required, RC fighter squadrons have a limited capacity to develop and absorb non-prior-service fighter pilots. Doing so requires multiple years of full-time training for what may likely be a part-time position. As discussed in Appendix C, many RC fighter pilot positions are already not filled. Thus, we see very limited potential for the RCs to support further mission increases.

Converting Nonabsorbing Positions to Absorbing

Converting nonabsorbing positions to absorbing would require a determination that certain requirements that heretofore have been filled exclusively by experienced fighter pilots could be partially filled by inexperienced pilots. Likely candidates would include aggressor, test, and FTU requirements. We would expect dilution of experience levels in these missions to increase risk in terms of both flying safety and mission effectiveness and would not consider it if other options are available.

Eliminating Requirements

There is some possibility that fighter pilot positions, particularly staff positions, could be eliminated outright. In response to a Department of Defense directive to reduce headquarters strengths by 20 percent, Air Force leaders plan to meet and possibly exceed that goal over the next five years (Department of the Air Force, "Air Force Announces Change to Headquarters Organization," 2014). Beyond that, we were unable to find an objective basis for evaluating the relative need for nonabsorbing cockpit positions for fighter pilots.[3] The Air Force manpower requirements process itself recognizes that management headquarters staffs have unique and changing requirements that have not been captured in standards or models (Robbert et al., 2014, p. 7). The approach typically used by the Air Force to reduce headquarters staff requirements is to arbitrarily allocate cuts to subordinate headquarters, allowing the subordinate headquarters to determine where to reduce their staffs.

While ongoing headquarters staff reductions might reduce some fighter pilot requirements, we do not recommend additional arbitrary cuts aimed specifically at fighter pilot positions. As discussed in Appendix F, past reductions have cut deeply into stated requirements for fighter pilots in headquarters staffs. While we have been unable to confirm that remaining requirements are valid, neither do we have a basis for concluding that remaining vacancies have no impact on effectiveness. A more prudent course, we believe, is the alternative discussed above, of converting some fighter pilot staff requirements to other workforce types.

---

[3] An analytic approach we considered was to identify positions that have been chronically unfilled. The Air Force personnel data system contains a field that can link a person to a specific position. However, we found that this field was too poorly maintained to permit a reliable analysis.

5. Paths Toward Balance

In this chapter, we evaluate combinations of the alternatives discussed in Chapters Three and Four that can lead to balancing fighter pilot absorption and sustainment, and hence eliminating expected fighter pilot shortfalls. We do not explicitly address training production, given that absorption capacity persistently below sustainment requirements has been the primary problem and on the assumption that resources can be made available to keep production capacity at or above absorption capacity.

In exploring these paths, we demonstrate that opportunities to increase supply are limited, perhaps to a greater degree than many decisionmakers realize. We calculate the magnitude of supply-side changes needed to eliminate shortage, primarily to demonstrate that the required magnitudes of change are beyond feasible bounds. This depiction of the limits of supply-side approaches supports our conclusion that reductions in demand are needed to restore balance to the system. Our ultimate recommendation is conversion of a specified number of fighter pilot staff requirements to other workforce types.

A Steady-State Approach

To ensure the adequacy of the various paths we construct, we need a convention for quantifying and depicting the expected results. In a complex system, in which the impacts of policy options play out over extended periods of time, steady-state analysis of alternatives is useful.[1] It allows analysts to readily explore many options individually and in combination. Here, we identify a long-range requirement, then depict the inventory that would be expected if current policies, approaches, and trends converged to a stable, steady-state outcome over a long period of time. We then assess how steady-state outcomes would vary from expected levels with different policy sets. From these analyses, we hope to identify a *strategy*—a set of plans, programs, policies, and practices that can be used to move the fighter aircrew management process toward balance while affording buffers large enough to accommodate year-to-year perturbations.

---

[1] One commonly used approach is to show excursions (dashed lines) from the expected solid-line demand and supply projections on a red-line/blue-line chart. We have not used that approach here, for several reasons. First, the red-line/blue-line charts require strict attention to the temporal dimension of policy changes, i.e., the timing of their implementation. We reasoned that in an early and open-ended review of policy options, timing is not a critical consideration. The shortfalls we are seeking to eliminate are long-range and persistent. The key consideration for a policy set at this stage of analysis is its feasibility and its adequacy rather than its immediacy. Second, the red-line/blue-line charts, with dashed-line excursions, tend to show ultimate impacts but do not readily reveal the multiple interactions of policy and environmental variables that produce those impacts.

Identifying a Long-Range Requirement

Recent AC fighter-pilot inventory projections are based on a decline in total fighter aircraft inventory, extending from FY 2016 to FY 2020, related to divestiture of the A-10 fleet prior to planned recapitalization through F-35 acquisitions. A suitable long-range target would be based on the FY 2023 projected AC aircraft inventory of 641 combat-coded fighters (Headquarters United States Air Force [AF/A3O-A], 2014) and a total requirement of about 3,450 AC fighter pilots.[2] As can be seen in Figure 1.1, requirements at this level provide a suitable long-range target.

Using the average number of hours that new pilots receive per month that count toward experience, AC units can absorb 0.22 inexperienced pilots per aircraft per year, or a total of 143 (0.22 times 641 aircraft) new pilots across the AC fleet.[3] A steady-state inventory equal to 3.05 pilots per AC aircraft could be sustained, or a total of 1,957 (3.05 pilots per aircraft times 641 aircraft) across the AC fleet. The nine inexperienced pilots absorbed each year in active associate cells will, with TARS of 14 years, sustain 126 additional pilots in the total inventory. The result is a baseline inventory of 2,083 (1,957 + 126) and a shortfall of 1,367. Required training production would be 152 (143 absorbed in AC units and nine absorbed in RC units) to meet AC needs and another 50 to 60 to meet RC needs.

To this we add the additional inventory sustainable by a modest level of simulator capacity (two simulator sorties per crew per month) in all units.[4] We believe it is reasonable to expect that simulators of the necessary quality will be included in programmed acquisitions in parallel with recapitalization of the fighter fleet. This would result in sustainable inventory of 3.46 per AC aircraft. This results in a projected long-term inventory of 2,215 plus the 126 from the associate units, for a total of 2,341. The shortfall is reduced to 1,109.

Increasing Supply

Increased Flying Hours and Simulator Usage

Increased flying hours and simulator usage would increase absorption capacity to the point that the total inventory requirement is sustainable. It would require a corresponding increase in training pipeline production.

Using the model described in Appendix A, we determined that increasing SCM from ten to slightly over 14, while also setting simulator hours at 20 percent of total hours credited toward the experienced level (the maximum under current fighter continuation training instructions,

---

[2] This figure includes 3,300 requirements conventionally included in red-line projections plus 150 nonpilot institutional requirements expected to be filled by fighter pilots.

[3] See the data included in Figure 2.2 and Base Case Step 1 in Table A.3.

[4] Identified as Base Case Step 2 in Table A.3.

produced by about five simulator sorties per month), and assuming the absorption capacity of five extant active associate units, would sustain the required inventory of 3,450.[5] However, two considerations militate against using this as the sole path to a solution. First, the flying-hour costs would be very high and likely beyond reach in a fiscally constrained environment. Second, if SCM reaches 14, the number of absorptions per squadron per year would be about nine. If initial operational tours were three years in length, 27 of a 24-PMAI unit's 30 RPI-1 pilots would be on their initial operational tours. This would leave inadequate opportunities for second operational tours by more senior pilots, resulting in an insufficient pool of pilots developed for squadron command and other supervisory positions and difficulty for pilots to fly sufficiently to maintain aviation incentive pay. See Taylor, Bigelow, and Ausink (2009) for a fuller discussion of the problems associated with insufficient opportunities for second operational tours. A more likely expectation is that live sortie production will remain at current levels but that simulator capacity will be increased to allow the maximum use of simulator hours in aging toward experienced levels.[6] This would increase absorption to 0.28 per aircraft per year, sustaining an inventory of 2,544, with a shortfall of 906.

Additional Active Associate Units

In Chapter Three, we documented an absorption capacity in five extant active associate units of nine inexperienced pilots per year, sustaining 126 pilots in the steady-state inventory. Current plans call for an additional 14 to 17 four-pilot associations, adding up to 17 additional absorptions per year and sustaining an additional 238 pilots in the long term inventory. If active associate units were the only available avenue for meeting fighter pilot shortfalls, a sustainable-inventory shortfall of 1,109 could be eliminated by increasing the existing and planned associations to 12 inexperienced pilots each. This would bring 24-PMAI RC squadrons very close to the conventional limit of 45 percent inexperienced pilots, but, unfortunately, would put 18-PMAI squadrons over the limit. A more likely outcome is that the planned associate units will materialize, increasing the inventory sustainable from this source from 126 to 364.

Increased First-Assignment Instructor Pilots

In our baseline, we assumed that the proportion of FAIPs in fighter pilot absorption would remain at 12 percent. Increasing the FAIP proportion would also increase absorption capacity—because they require less aging—and would also increase the sustainable inventory, although to a lesser degree than the increase in absorption capacity because FAIPs have reduced fighter-specific TARS. An AETC source advised us that the undergraduate flying training community can absorb (and hence rotate out) about 80 FAIPs per year, of which 30 are currently earmarked

---

[5] Excursion 1 in Table A.3.

[6] Air Force policy currently permits 20 percent of hours credited toward the 500-hour experienced benchmark to be gained in simulators.

for fighters. Given the interests of other aviation communities, but relying on its unique absorption constraints, the fighter community might be able to claim 60 of the 80 FAIPs per year, doubling the FAIP input to fighter squadrons. Applied to our baseline case, doubling fighter FAIP absorption could increase absorption from 0.22 to 0.24 per year for squadrons without appropriate simulator capability, yielding a total inventory of 2,155 and a shortfall of 1,029.[7]

Increased Retention

Due to an expected surge in airline retirements, the near-term prospects for increased fighter pilot retention are limited. However, to illustrate the potential impacts of improved retention, we calculated the sustainable inventory if our assumed TARS of 14 years were to increase to 16 years. This level of TARS may be optimistic, but, as indicated in Figure 3.1, during several multiyear periods it was either exceeded or nearly equaled. Applied to our baseline case, the sustainable inventory would increase to 2,370, reducing the shortfall to 1,081.[8]

Using Reservists to Meet AC Requirements

The potential contribution of this approach is limited by fighter pilot shortfalls in the RC, which proportionally exceed those of the AC, as noted in Appendix C. Before assuming large-scale availability of RC fighter pilots to meet AC requirements, the RCs will have to find ways to increase affiliation of separating AC pilots, which are already at a high level, or to absorb more non-prior-service pilots. We note that in Aircrew Summit 2014 materials (Headquarters United States Air Force [AF/A3/5 Reserve Advisor], 2014), the Air Staff proposed filling only ten fighter pilot staff positions using reservists on MPA man-days.

Net Effect of Potential Supply-Side Alternatives

The net effect of the alternatives discussed above is not additive. We estimate the combined effects using the approach described in detail in Appendix A. In making our estimates, we assume the following:

- The AC fighter fleet will total 641 aircraft.
- Live sortie production will remain at current levels (10 SCM), with 1.4 hours average sortie duration, but simulator capacity will be increased to allow maximum use (20 percent of creditable hours) in aging toward experienced levels.
- Four eight-pilot and 15 four-pilot active associate units will each be absorbing two and one pilots, respectively, per year.
- 24 percent of fighter absorptions (double the current proportion) will be FAIPs.
- TARS will be 16 years.

---

[7] Excursion 3 in Table A.3; similar figures for units with simulator capability are shown in excursion 4 .

[8] Excursion 5 in Table A.3.

- 10 reservists will fill AC requirements.

With these assumptions, the total annual AC fighter pilot absorption level is 188 pilots in AC units and 23 pilots in active associate units.[9] The sustainable fighter pilot inventory is 3,250, leaving a shortfall of 200. This remaining shortfall can be eliminated by increasing the fighter utilization rates such that SCM could rise from 10 to 10.8.[10] On the other hand, if SCM were raised to this level but retention remained at recent levels (TARS = 14 years), the steady-state shortfall would be about 400.[11]

One cautionary note is that these excursions would result in 7 to 7.5 absorptions per year in each squadron. With three-year tours, that would result in 21 to 23 of a squadron's 30 pilots being on their first operational tour. Opportunities for second operational tours, as with other enhanced-absorption alternatives discussed above, might be insufficient.

We conclude that a further reduction of about 400 nonabsorbing fighter pilot requirements is needed. This will allow sustainment needs to be met, generally with some slack, over a range of retention and utilization rates.

Reducing Demand

As indicated in Chapter Four, we were unable to identify a process to independently prioritize fighter staff requirements or to discern which requirements could be cut or, much more preferably, filled by other than AC fighter pilots. However, RSAP target manning levels reflect the prioritization of these requirements by senior Air Force leadership. An acceptable approach, we believe, is to allocate targets for converting AC fighter pilot positions to other types of personnel according to the targeted manning levels in the FY 2014 RSAP. This will require additional judgments within the affected organizations to determine which specific positions would be converted.

Increasing Demand with a Leveraged Increase in Supply

Each 24-PMAI squadron increase in the AC would increase fighter pilot requirements by 30 API-1 pilots, plus about ten API-6 pilots,[12] but would increase long-run steady-state inventory by about 75 to 125 pilots, depending on which other options and conditions outlined above were in effect. If the assumptions in the last supply-side case described above were to hold, the change in sustainable inventory would be a gain of about 60 per added 24-PMAI AC squadron and a loss of about 14 per reduced 18-PMAI RC squadron. The 400-pilot shortfall remaining in that

---

[9] Excursion 6 in Table A.3.

[10] Excursion 7 in Table A.3.

[11] Excursion 8 in Table A.3.

[12] Estimate of 10 API-6 pilots per squadron is based on an overall ratio of about 3:1 between API-1 fighter positions (1,400, as of September 2014 in the AFPC IDEAS database) and API-6 fighter positions (479).

excursion would be eliminated with eleven additional 24-PMAI squadrons in the AC, equivalent in force structure to fourteen 18-PMAI squadrons in the RCs.

Clearly, as reflected in the report of the National Commission on the Structure of the Air Force (2014) and in the subsequent public statements of senior Air Force leaders (Department of the Air Force, "Great Deal of Symmetry Between AF, National Commission Recommendations," 2014), there is a consensus against shifting the future force mix toward the AC. Additionally there would likely be considerable organizational and political obstacles to implementing such changes, such as occurred when the Air Force unveiled its plans for force structure changes with its FY 2013 budget submission. Nonetheless, an important long-run outcome of such a shift would be reduced fighter pilot shortfalls in both AC staff positions and RC cockpit positions. The AC would benefit, in the long run, from the increase in the supply of fighter pilots exceeding the increase in demand. The RCs would benefit because, in the long run and all else equal, a larger AC pilot inventory would result in more pilots separating from the AC and available for affiliation, while at the same time reducing the number of units across which to spread the available affiliations.

Cost is inevitably a consideration in force mix decisions. Robbert (2013) demonstrated that, when flying-hour costs fully loaded with personnel and support costs were considered, costs per flying hour in an AC F-16 wing were about the same as in an RC wing. The key to minimizing total costs of the fleet, according to this study, was to find the AC/RC mix that minimized the demand for flying hours. Line units face two categories of demand for flying hours: operational sorties in support of combatant commanders and training sorties to round out whatever flying proficiency requirements cannot be met while flying operational sorties. RC and AC units differ in their opportunities to fly operational sorties as well as in the amount of proficiency flying they require in addition to their operational sorties. For the F-16 fleet, Robbert (2013) found that a shift in the mix of the F-16 fleet toward a greater proportion in the AC would have reduced total fleet flying hours, and hence costs, in the period studied (FYs 2006 to 2010), although the savings would have been minimal.[13]

We note that a shift in the force mix can be effected without moving force structure from the RCs to the AC, by taking future force structure reductions more heavily from the RCs than from the AC, thus avoiding transition costs that would be incurred in moving existing PMAI from one component to another. The aircrew management benefits are significant enough, we believe, to warrant a close examination of the cost implications, which likely fall somewhere between slightly unfavorable and slightly favorable, of shifting the mix toward the AC. A more modest

---

[13] The study found that the fleet of combat-coded F-16s averaged 660 PMAI during the period studied, with 52 percent of the fleet in the AC. The fleet consumed an average of 181,500 flying hours per year. The cost-minimizing mix would have been with 64 percent of the fleet in the AC, consuming 172,300 flying hours per year. Had the fleet been at the cost-minimizing mix, estimated savings would have been $60 million per year—only 1.4 percent of the fleet's $4.4 billion annual cost.

proposal would be to shift the mix enough to eliminate persistent fighter pilot shortages in the RCs.

Continued Attention to Aircrew Management Dynamics

The primary source of stress in fighter-pilot management has been reductions in aircraft inventories leading to reductions in absorption capacity that are less than sustainment needs, and at times also less than actual training production. A reduction of 400 nonabsorbing requirements, or less if combined with a measured shift of force structure to the AC, could provide a reasonable prospect of the system becoming balanced in the long run. With favorable retention and/or aircraft utilization rate trends, the system might also reach a healthy level of buffering capacity.

We do not advocate a policy of strictly limiting demand to the expected supply in every time period. To do so would make requirements, particularly staff requirements, more volatile than is necessary. However, once the system is rebalanced, it is possible that unfavorable trends in aircraft inventories, utilization rates, pilot retention, and other related factors could again make stated requirements unsustainable. The Air Force's interests will be best served by remaining alert to the possibility that unfavorable trends have become unalterable and, should that occur, again making adjustments to balance production, absorption, and sustainment.

Appendix A: Fighter Squadron Absorption Capacity

This appendix provides a method for calculating the absorption capacity of an AC fighter squadron (Table A.1) and extending it to an Air Force-wide level (Table A.2). In practice, the inputs and calculations shown in these tables are embedded in an Excel spreadsheet that can be used as a what-if tool to vary and gauge the sensitivity of the factors that influence absorption. In Tables A.1 and A.2, inputs are unshaded, while calculations are shaded in gray.

Table A.1. Calculating Unit Absorption Capacity

Factor	Calculation	Value
Unit Configuration		
PMAI		24
Crew ratio		1.25
Crew strength	PAA * crew ratio	30
Required experience level		55%
Inexperienced strength	Crew strength * (1 − required experience level)	13.5
Aging Rate		
Ready Aircrew Program (RAP) live sorties per crew per month		10
RAP simulator sorties per crew per month		0
Total RAP sorties per crew per month	Live sorties + simulator sorties	10
Average live sortie duration (hours)		1.4
Average simulator sortie duration (hours)		1
Live sortie hours per crew per month	Live sorties * live sortie duration	14
Simulator hours per crew per month	Simulator sorties * simulator sortie duration	0
Creditable hours per crew per month	Simulator hours + live sortie hours	14
Non-FAIP Aging Requirements		
Fighter hours required to reach experienced level		500
FTU hours		80
Required hours to experienced in operational unit	Fighter hours to experienced − FTU hours	420
Months of flying to reach experienced level in operational unit	Required hours to experienced in operational unit / creditable hours per crew per month	30.00
Months not available to fly (Squadron Officer School, etc.)		2
Total months to experienced level	Months of flying + months not available to fly	32

33

Factor	Calculation	Value
Years to experienced level in operational unit	Months to experienced level / 12	2.67

FAIP Aging Requirements

Factor	Calculation	Value
Fighter hours required to reach experienced level		300
FTU hours		80
Required hours to experienced in operational unit	Fighter hours to experienced − FTU hours	220
Months of flying to reach experienced level in operational unit	Required hours to experienced in operational unit / creditable hours per crew per month	15.71
Months not available to fly (Squadron Officer School, etc.)		1
Total months to experienced level	Months of flying + months not available to fly	16.71
Years to experienced level in operational unit	Months to experienced level / 12	1.39

Absorption Capacity

Factor	Calculation	Value
FAIP proportion in in fighter B-course distribution[a]		12%
Total annual absorptions[b]	Let X = total annual absorptions. Solve for X.	5.37
	(X * Non-FAIP proportion * Non-FAIP years to experienced level) + (X * FAIP proportion * FAIP years to experienced level) = Inexperienced strength (where inexperienced strength is calculated as in Unit Configuration section above)	
	Using figures derived above:	
	(X * 0.88 * 2.67) + (X * 0.12 * 1.39) = 13.5	
	X = 5.37	
Annual Non-FAIP absorptions	Total annual absorptions * (1 - FAIP proportion)	4.73
Annual FAIP absorptions	Total annual absorptions * FAIP proportion	0.64
Non-FAIP inexperienced strength	Non-FAIP absorptions * Non-FAIP years to experienced level	12.6
FAIP inexperienced strength	FAIP absorptions * FAIP years to experienced level	.9
Total inexperienced strength	Non-FAIP inexperienced strength + FAIP inexperienced strength (as a cross-check on these calculations, should equal inexperienced strength from Unit Configuration section)	13.5
Total annual absorption per PMAI	Total absorptions/PAA	0.22

NOTES:
a. Based on 30 FAIPs per year in annual distribution of approximately 250 B-course graduates to the AC.
b. Fractions of a person, as shown in these computations, represent steady-state averages over multiple units and multiple time periods.

Table A.2. Calculating Total Sustainable Inventories

Factor	Calculation	Value
Squadron-Level Sustainable Inventory from Non-FAIPs		
Non-FAIP absorptions in 24-PMAI squadron	From Table A.1	4.73
Fighter-specific TARS (non-FAIP)		14
Sustainable inventory	Absorptions x TARS	66.2
Squadron-Level Sustainable Inventory from FAIPs		
FAIP absorptions in 24-PMAI squadron	From Table A.1	.64
FAIP tour length (years)		3
Fighter-specific TARS (FAIP)	Non-FAIP TARS - FAIP tour length	11
Sustainable inventory	Absorptions x TARS	7.0
Total Sustainable Inventory from AC PMAI		
Total sustainable inventory per 24-PMAI squadron	Non-FAIP sustainable inventory + FAIP sustainable inventory	73.3
Sustainable inventory per PMAI	Total sustainability inventory per 24-PMAI squadron / 24	3.05
AC fleet size (total PMAI)		641
Total sustainable inventory from AC PMAI	Total PMAI x sustainable inventory per PMAI	1,957
Sustainable Inventory from Active Associate Units		
Associate unit absorptions		9
Sustainable inventory	Absorptions x TARS	126
Total Sustainable Inventory		
Total	Sustainable inventory from AC PMAI + sustainable inventory from active associate units	2,082

The "Base Case Step 1" section of Table A.3 summarizes key pieces of information for the base case corresponding to the values in Tables A.1 and A.2 and also includes two more values: The column labeled "Total Steady-State Absorb in 641 AC Aircraft" shows that AC units can absorb 143 pilots per year (0.22 absorbed per aircraft times 641). The production pipeline must provide these 143 pilots plus the nine pilots that are to be absorbed in active associate units. This leads to the value 152 in the column labeled "Total AC Pipeline Production Requirement."

An excursion from the results shown in Tables A.1 and A.2 would add simulator sorties in the calculation of the aging rate. An addition of two simulator sorties per month (yielding creditable simulator aging that is well within the allowable 20 percent of experienced hours) would increase total absorptions from 5.37 to 6.08 (from 0.22 absorptions per aircraft per year to 0.25). Excursion 1 in Table A.3 shows the impacts.

Absorption capacity is also sensitive to the proportion of FAIPs among inexperienced pilots entering operational units. In the calculations presented in Table A.1, doubling the FAIP proportion to 24 percent would result in total annual absorptions increasing from 5.37 (base case in Table A.3) to 5.72 (excursion 4 in Table A.3), a not-insubstantial 6.5 percent increase in absorption capacity. This benefit, however, is partially offset by the fewer years of fighter-specific TARS supplied by FAIPs. Their expected fighter-specific TARS would be less than that of non-FAIPS by the length of their FAIP tour. Assuming that training production could be increased to match improved absorption capacity, Table A.3 demonstrates that doubling the FAIP proportion would, in the steady state, increase the fighter pilot inventory generated by the unit's absorptions from 73.3 to 76.0—a 3.7 percent increase (excursion 4 in Table A.3). Combining additional simulator credit of 2 hours per month with a doubled FAIP proportion would result in an inventory increase from 73.3 to 85.9—a 17.2 percent increase (excursion 5 in Table A.3).

The full set of excursions depicted in Table A.3 corresponds to the paths explored in Chapter Five.

Table A.3. Impact of Aircrew Management Options on Absorption Capacity and Sustainable Inventories

	Annual Unit Absorb[a]	Annual Absorb Per Aircraft	Fighter-Specific TARS[b]	Steady-State Inventory Generated by Unit's Absorption[c]	Sustainable Steady-State Inventory per AC Aircraft	Total Steady-state Absorb in 641 AC Acft	Total AC Pipeline Production Rqmt[d]	Total Steady-State Inventory With 641 AC Aircraft	Total Steady-State Inventory Including Sustainment from Associate Units	Shortfall Against 3,450 Total Inventory Requirements
Base Case Step 1 – 12% FAIPS, no simulator sorties, 9 absorptions per year in active associate units										
Non-FAIPs	4.73		14	66.2						
FAIPs	.64		11	7.0						
Total	5.37	.22		73.3	3.05	143	152	1,957	2,083	1,367
Base Case Step 2 – 12% FAIPs, 2 simulator sorties per month, 9 absorptions per year in active associate units										
Non-FAIPs	5.35		14	74.9						
FAIPs	.73		11	8.0						
Total	6.08	.25		82.9	3.46	162	171	2,215	2,341	1,109
Excursion 1 – 12% FAIPs, 20% of experiencing hours in simulators, live SCM increased as necessary to meet sustainment requirements (14.25 SCM), 9 absorptions per year in active associate units										
Non-FAIPs	8.03		14	112.4						
FAIPs	1.09		11	12.0						
Total	9.12	.38		124.5	5.18	244	253	3,324	3,450	0
Excursion 2 – 12% FAIPs, 20% of experiencing hours in simulators, live sortie production at current level (10 SCM), 9 absorptions per year in active associate units										
Non-FAIPs	5.82		14	81.4						
FAIPs	0.79		11	8.7						
Total	6.61	.28		90.2	3.75	177	186	2,408	2,544	906
Excursion 3 – 24% FAIPs, no simulator sorties, 9 absorptions per year in active associate units										
Non-FAIPs	4.35		14	60.9						
FAIPs	1.37		11	15.1						
Total	5.72	.24		76.0	3.17	153	162	2,029	2,155	1,295
Excursion 4 – 24% FAIPs, 2 simulator sorties per month, 9 absorptions per year in active associate units										
Non-FAIPs	4.92		14	68.9						
FAIPs	1.55		11	17.1						
Total	6.48	.27		85.9	3.58	173	182	2,295	2,421	1,029
Excursion 5 – 12% FAIPs, no simulator sorties, 9 absorptions per year in active associate units, increased retention (TARS = 16 years)										
Non-FAIPs	4.73		16	75.7						
FAIPs	.64		13	8.3						
Total	5.37	.22		84.0	3.5	143	152	2,244	2,370	1,081

	Annual Unit Absorb[a]	Annual Absorb Per Aircraft	Fighter-Specific TARS[b]	Steady-State Inventory Generated by Unit's Absorption[c]	Sustainable Steady-State Inventory per AC Aircraft	Total Steady-state Absorb in 641 AC Acft	Total AC Pipeline Production Rqmt[d]	Total Steady-State Inventory With 641 AC Aircraft	Total Steady-State Inventory Including Sustainment from Associate Units	Shortfall Against 3,450 Total Inventory Requirements
Excursion 6 – 24% FAIPs, 20% of experiencing hours in simulators, live sortie production at current level (10 SCM), 23 absorptions per year in active associate units, increased retention (TARS = 16 years); 10 reservists fill AC staff requirements										
Non-FAIPs	5.35		16	85.6						
FAIPs	1.69		13	22.0						
Total	7.04	.29		107.5	4.5	188	211	2,872	3,250[e]	200
Excursion 7 – Same as Excursion 6, except SCM = 10.8										
Non-FAIPs	5.63		16	90.1						
FAIPs	1.78		13	23.1						
Total	7.41	.31		113.2	4.7	198	221	3,024	3,450[e]	0
Excursion 8 – Same as Excursion 6, except SCM = 10.8 and TARS = 14 years										
Non-FAIPs	5.63		14	78.8						
FAIPs	1.78		11	19.6						
Total	7.41	.31		98.4	4.1	198	221	2,628	3,048[e]	402

NOTES:
- a. Developed using the inputs and calculations as shown in Table A.1.
- b. Fourteen years is a rough average for fighter pilots. Fighter-specific TARs is reduced for FAIPS by the length of a FAIP tour, assumed to be about three years.
- c. Steady-state inventory attributable to the unit's absorptions = annual absorption * fighter-specific TARS.
- d. Total force production requirement would also include RC requirements, likely to be in the range of 50 to 60 per year (based on recent history—see Figure D.2). To provide appropriate buffers, total force production capacity should exceed AC and RC combined requirements while actual production should be at or close to absorption capacity.
- e. Includes 10 reservists filling staff positions using MPA man-days.

Appendix B: RAND's Total Force Blue Line Model

Recognizing that aircrew management throughout the total force would benefit from greater coordination among the active and reserve components, the Air Force Chief of staff, at a 2013 Rated Summit, directed the formation of a Total Force Aircrew Management (TFAM) office. Critical to the success of TFAM formation is a capability to generate reliable, consistent projections of aircrew requirements (represented by red lines on the resulting graphics) and inventories (represented by blue lines) and to assess the impact of policy changes on these projections. The AC has well-developed analytic capability to generate its red-line/blue-line projections. For inventory projections, it has its Air Force Rated Aircrew Management System (AFRAMS) model, while capabilities in the RCs were more limited—lacking, for example, the capability to project either expected or policy-driven changes in inventories over time.

RAND has developed a modeling capability—its Total Force Blue Line model—that can satisfy this need. As part of its support for rated management activities during FY 2014, PAF worked with the emergent TFAM staff to update and apply this model. This appendix describes the essential elements of the model.

These estimates begin with a set of inventory levels from the Air Force personnel files. The model then estimates inventories for subsequent years using a simple conservation equation: The inventory of any rated category at the end of a fiscal year equals the inventory at the end of the previous year, plus gains during the year minus losses during the year. The model estimates inventory categories that cover each component (AC, ANG, AFR), crew position (pilot, combat system officer, air battle manager, and RPA operator), and major weapon system—nearly 60 categories in all. The model considers the usual types of gains and losses: new officers who complete undergraduate training and earn their wings, officers who separate from AC and leave military service, officers who leave the rated inventory (such as promotion to O-6) but remain in the AC, officers who separate from the AC and affiliate with an RC (both a gain and a loss), and other transfers of officers in and out of the force or between inventory categories. The model tracks these gains and losses for each component, estimating separation and affiliation rates from historical baselines.

Though the model focuses on rated inventories, requirements must also be considered. These are the funded authorizations for rated personnel—the jobs that rated officers perform. Requirements are inputs to the model, provided by the Air Force MPES. By comparing inventory projections with requirements, to determine how well available inventories meet the requirements for pilots, it is possible to gauge the health of the rated inventory. The model has sufficient flexibility to allow the user to assign inventory categories to requirements categories and to prioritize those assignments. These "assignments" then allow the model to use surplus inventory in one category to fill shortfalls in another, according to business rules defined by the user. It also has the capability to allow rated officers from one component to fill inventory requirements in another.

The inventory conservation equation at the heart of the model takes the following form:

$$Inv(icat, cy, fy) = Inv(icat, cy - 1, fy - 1)$$
$$+Gains(icat, cy, fy) - Losses(icat, cy, fy)$$
$$+ \sum_{jcat} [Trans(jcat, icat, cy, fy) - Trans(icat, jcat, cy, fy)]$$

Where:

- *Inv (icat, cy, fy)* represents the inventory in a cell, defined by *icat* = inventory category, *cy* = commissioned year of service, and *fy* = fiscal year.
- *Gains (icat, cy, fy)* represents additions from outside the system such as production of new rated officers;
- *Losses (icat, cy, fy)* represents officers leaving the system;
- *Trans (icat, jcat, cy, fy)* represents the transition of officers from one inventory category (*icat*) to another (*jcat*). This is a loss from inventory category *icat* and a gain to category *jcat*.

The primary source of gains is training production. The model relies on user specification of production in each *icat* and *fy*, but distributes the gains to *cy* using historical rates. Although other types of gains are possible (e.g., rated recalls), the model does not include them.

Losses are estimated using historical attrition rates, averaged over appropriate periods. As expected, attrition patterns differ significantly between the AC and RCs. Figures B.1 and B.2 illustrate the loss patterns for various categories of pilots in the AC and RCs. The AC patterns are driven by the initial active duty service commitment (which was extended to ten years during the period covered in this figure) and the immediate annuity available at 20 years of service. In contrast, the RC patterns have no such spikes.

TARS, and the RC equivalent, is computed as the sum of annual probabilities that a gain will remain in a respective inventory.

The Air Force's AFRAMS model uses *bonus take rates* as an input in estimating attrition, allowing attrition rates to vary across *fy*'s as a function of user-estimated changes in bonus take rates. The user can, if he or she wishes, provide the RAND model with attrition rates that vary by year, in order to match TARS to those derived in AFRAMS.

The most important set of transitions in the model is affiliation of separating AC officers with one of the RCs. The model constrains affiliations to be less than or equal to the eligible officers separating from active duty, subject to user-specified constraints on which AC categories can supply officers to each AFR or ANG category. The model may be run using historical rates at which separating officers affiliate with the AFR or ANG, or it may be run to determine the affiliation rates needed to fill AFR and ANG requirements. Historical affiliation rates for fighter and mobility pilots are shown in Figure B.3.

Figure B.1. Historical Attrition Rates of AC Fighter and Other Pilots (FYs 2004–2013)

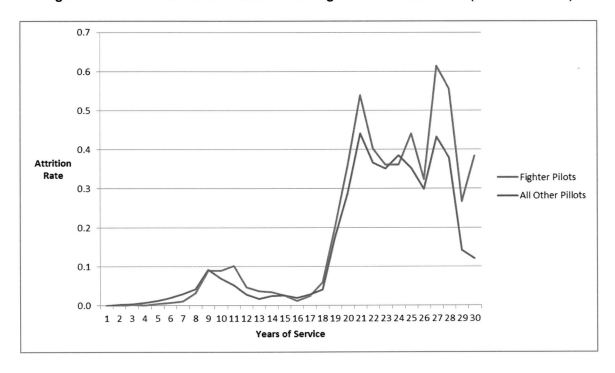

Figure B.2. Historical Attrition Rates of RC Fighter and Mobility Pilots (FYs 2004–2013)

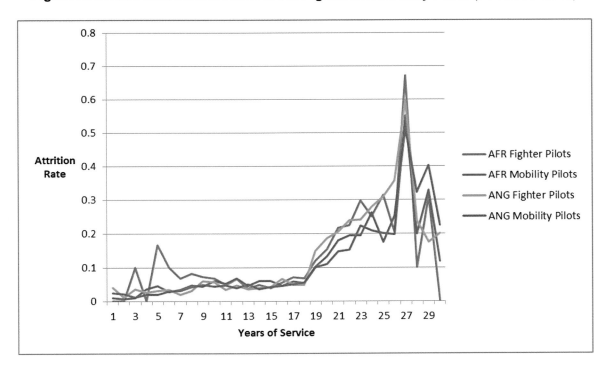

Figure B.3. Historical Pilot Affiliation Rates (FYs 2004–2013)

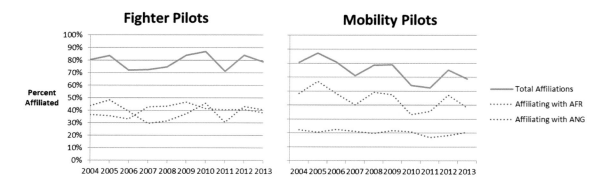

NOTE: Affiliation rates are for AC pilots separating with less than 17 years of service and affiliating with an RC unit within six years of separation.

In constructing inventory projections, the model allows for some cross-utilization among categories. As examples, any AC inventory category can be used against an *unspecified* rated requirement, or any AC pilot category can be shown as assigned against an RPA requirement.

Effective utilization of the model requires support from an analytic staff and user communities and a customer for its outputs. Support from an analytic staff is needed to, for example, update attrition and other key rates or to implement policy alternatives in the model. Support from user communities is needed to provide input parameters, such as training production, and user-specified constraints. Finally, the resources needed to maintain and operate the model will be forthcoming only if there is an interested customer for its outputs. Such interest in maximizing total force aircrew assets would have to come from the TFAM Office and senior leadership within both the AC and the RCs.

Appendix C: Pilot Shortages in RC Fighter Units

In the course of investigating the use of RC officers to fill AC fighter pilot positions, it became apparent that the RCs were also suffering from a shortage of fighter pilots. Undermanning in the ANG appears greater than in the AFR. To investigate this issue further, we examined historical data from the manpower requirements reflected in the MPES against annual personnel data obtained from the AFPC at the individual level of detail. For each of the installations listed, we used the unique Personnel Accounting Symbol (PAS) codes associated with that installation to pull both the ANG requirements for fighter pilots from the MPES data and the actual ANG personnel at that installation with either a duty or primary AFSC of fighter pilot. Using these data, we are able to compare historic manning levels versus requirements for each of these installations. As indicated in Table C.1, many ANG fighter squadrons have pilot manning levels of 80 percent or less.

Causes, issues, and potential solutions of undermanning differ between the AC and RCs. The RCs have much less centralized personnel management functions; notably, recruiting and hiring are squadron/group-level rather than central management responsibilities. Factors that may influence RC undermanning include regularity of recruiting and sending pilots to SUPT, deployment frequency, the presence of an ACA mission, and flying-hour allocation processes. This appendix briefly describes the differences in manning processes between the AC and RC unit manning and describes how the aforementioned factors may impact unit manning.

Unique Elements of RC Unit Manning

Manning responsibilities and processes in an RC unit are substantially different from an AC unit. In an AC wing, unit commanders regularly work with the AFPC to reassign and gain new pilots. Corporate Air Force processes and policies ensure a steady flow of personnel to man AC line fighter units at 100 percent. In RC units, commanders are generally responsible for recruiting to meet their unit's requirements. Unlike the AC, which relies on, and is beholden to AFPC, there is very little corporate infrastructure supporting RC pilot hiring. Even though in-service recruiters are part of the process when pilots transfer from the AC, the recruitment and hiring decision is ultimately made by the hiring RC unit.

RC units gain personnel through two sources: affiliations of separated AC personnel and accession of personnel directly into RC units. Pilots affiliating have typically completed their active duty service commitment and come to a mutual agreement with the hiring unit to continue to serve. Direct accessions must meet the prerequisite criteria for becoming an officer and pilot. These direct hires often, but not always, have some military experience, either officer or enlisted.

It appears more common in ANG units to commission enlisted personnel already serving in the unit.

Pilots affiliating from active duty have already been trained as pilots and, since they are likely already mission-ready in the RC unit's aircraft type, quickly contribute as mission-ready members in the RC unit. Affiliating pilots who are not trained in the RC unit's aircraft require transition training. Obtaining these transition training courses is sometimes an obstacle because the courses are limited in number, shared between the RCs and the AC, and must be planned for as part of FTU scheduling and resourcing.

Factors That Affect Unit Manning Levels

To better understand the possible causes of low fighter pilot manning in RC units, we examined the data in Table C.1 and also visited several units. We considered the following possibilities.

Flying-Hour Allocation

The ANG allocates flying hours to its units based on current unit manning, not PMAI or authorized manning. The basis for allocating flying hours in this manner is that a fixed number of flying hours are assumed to be needed per pilot to maintain combat mission–ready status under the ready aircrew program. This method of allocating flying hours seems to counter one often-heard explanation for RC fighter unit undermanning—that units claim flying-hour funding and other resources based on full manning, but intentionally underman in order to shift resources to other purposes.

ACA Mission

As of September 2014, there were 16 ANG fighter units that had an ACA mission. This air defense mission includes approximately ten to 12 full-time AGR positions in each squadron. Since AGR positions are typically easier to fill than part-time drill-status reservist positions, some have suggested that having an ACA mission contributes to higher manning.

Harder-to-Fill Part-Time Billets

RC units contain both full-time and part-time members. Full-time members are either AGRs or technicians. AGR status is very similar to full-time active duty in that the same retirement benefits apply for members reaching 20 years of service. Drill-status reservists serve on a part-time basis and often have other employment as their full-time job. In most units, it is the part-time positions that are vacant, with both the technician and AGR positions being easier to man because of the attractive pay and benefits.

Table C.1. Selected ANG Fighter Unit Manning Levels, SUPT Inputs, and ACA Mission

Location	RC Component	Unit	MDS	Six-Year Manning Average (%)	ACA Mission	Expected SUPT Graduates FY 2011–2016[a]
Joint Base Peral Harbor-Hickam, HI	ANG	154 W	F-22	106	X	6
Joint Base Langley-Eustis, VA	ANG	192d FW	F-22	97		1
Toledo Express Airport, OH	ANG	180th FW	F-16	95	X	9
Gowen Field, Idaho	ANG	124th W	A-10	95		7
Martin State Airport, Maryland	ANG	175th W	A-10	94		6
Joint Base San Antonio, TX	ANG	149th FW	F-16	93		2
Tucson International Airport, AZ	ANG	162d FW	F-16	87	X	12
Montgomery Regional Airport, AL	ANG	187th FW	F-16	87		7
Colorado ANG, Buckley AFB, Aurora, Colorado	ANG	140 W	F-16	86	X	1
Joe Foss Field, Sioux Falls, SD	ANG	114th FW	F-16	84	X	12
Burlington International Airport, VT	ANG	158th FW	F-16	82	X	11
Portland International Airport, OR	ANG	142d FW	F-15C	82	X	11
McEntire Air National Guard Station, SC	ANG	169th FW	F-16	81		6
Kingsley Field, Klamath Falls, OR	ANG	173d FW	F-15C	80		3
Fort Wayne International Airport, IN	ANG	122d FW	F-16	80		1
Duluth International Airport, MN	ANG	148th FW	F-16	80	X	15
Atlantic City International Airport, NJ	ANG	177th FW	F-16	77	X	8
Jacksonville International Airport, FL	ANG	125th FW	F-15C	76	X	3
NAS New Orleans, LA	ANG	159th FW	F-15C	75	X	11
Barnes ANG Base, MA	ANG	104th FW	F-15C	75	X	9
Des Moines International Airport, IA	ANG	132d FW	F-16	72		5
Fort Smith Regional Airport, AK	ANG	188th FW	A-10	69		9
Selfridge Air National Guard Base, MI	ANG	127th W	A-10	68		9
Great Falls International Airport, MT	ANG	120th FW	F-15C	64		6
NAS Fort. Worth/JRB Carswell, TX	AFRC	301st FW	F-16	97		1*
Hill AFB, UT	AFRC	419th FW	F-16	100		1*
Homestead Air Reserve Base, FL	AFRC	482nd FW	F-16	97		4*
Luke AFB, AZ	AFRC	944th FW	F-16	73		0*

NOTE: FW = fighter wing.
a. Number in pipeline as of June 2014.

Direct accessions must go through a much longer training process before returning to the hiring unit as qualified pilots. Training required for these hires may include officer training school, flight screening, SUPT, IFF, FTU, and survival training. Depending on the specific courses required and the training course start dates, it takes between two and three years for a hired member to return to the unit as an initially trained pilot basically qualified in the unit's aircraft. For expected ANG fighter SUPT graduations between FY 2010 and FY 2014, 188 members started into the training pipeline and 166 finished for an 86 percent completion rate.

Unit Location

Another postulated factor that influences manning is the location of the unit. Ideally, units would be located near a large population center and be co-located with a major airline hub to facilitate the participation of part-time reservists who are also airline pilots. RC units in less populated areas not near a major airline hub would presumably be more difficult to man fully.

Deployments

Another factor contributing to manning is the frequency of unit deployments. Frequent deployment may cause members to serve less time in the RCs to avoid repeated deployments. Conversely, units that have a deployment commitment may be more motivated to fully man their rosters to both meet their deployment commitments and to prevent unit members from going on repeated deployments.

Tentative Conclusions

The data in Table C.1 can be used to determine whether some of these factors are actually related to pilot undermanning. The table shows the number of SUPT inputs from the unit and the presence of an ACA mission. We find that a high level of manning is not strongly correlated with either having an ACA mission or consistent SUPT inputs. Probably the most that we can say is that F-16 units with an ACA mission and consistent SUPT inputs are generally better manned than other units. However, Duluth and San Antonio would appear to be exceptions. Duluth has both an ACA mission and the highest number of SUPT inputs but has a relatively low manning level. Conversely San Antonio lacks an ACA mission, has sent only two pilots to SUPT in the past five years, but has one of the highest average manning levels.

Given the two sources of inputs to ANG fighter units—affiliation and direct accessions—improvements in pilot manning in RC fighter units will probably require an increase in direct accessions. Recent affiliation rates for fighter pilots are shown in Figure B.3. These rates are appreciably higher than those observed in most other Air Force career fields and may be difficult to elevate further. While direct accessions present challenges, as discussed above, increasing this source may provide a more feasible path toward healthy RC unit manning than increasing affiliations.

Appendix D: Impacts of Fighter Force Structure Reductions on Fighter Pilot Inventory Management

This appendix provides a historical perspective on how fighter force structure reductions over the past several decades have reduced the Air Force's capacity to generate total fighter pilot inventories of sufficient size to cover all requirements. It is supplemented by Appendix E, which provides a chronology of key aircrew management decisions during those decades.

Fighter Force Structure Reductions

Figure D.1 shows the reduction in PMAI aircraft available to operational units occurring since the Cold War drawdown. For much of this period, the Air Force's capacity to balance its fighter pilot management dynamics suffered significantly, as programming decisions eliminated buffers and generated difficult operational realities for fighter units. Budget-driven programming decisions continued to generate sizable force structure reductions, while fighter pilot production goals exceeded absorption capacities.

Figure D.1. Total Force Fighter Inventory (FYs 1990–2013)

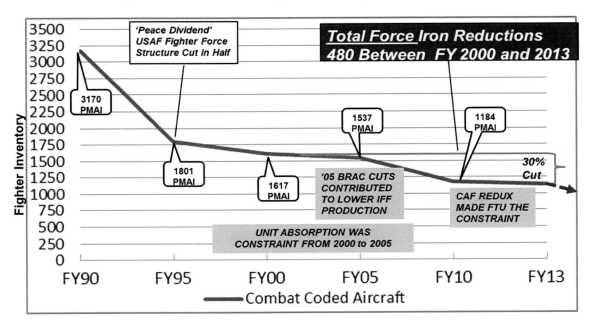

SOURCE: Headquarters United States Air Force (AF/A3O-A), "Alt FY15 POM Fighter Impacts and Recommendations," 2013.

The steady decrease in total force fighter PMAI continued throughout the 2000s after the sizable post–Cold War force structure cuts that removed nearly 50 percent of fighter PMAI during the 1990s. The total force PMAI reductions since FY 2000, broken down by component, are shown in Table D.1, which shows a decrease of 30. During this same period, fighter pilot (11F) requirements for all organizations, not just fighter units, declined by only 19 percent (from 4,223 to 3,421) (Headquarters United States Air Force [AF/A30-A], 2013). Thus, absorption capacity decreased faster than pilot inventory requirements, resulting in dynamic imbalances.

Table D.1. Total Force Fighter PMAI (FYs 2000–2013)

Component	FY 2000	FY 2005	FY 2010	FY 2013	% Decrease
AC	994	932	692	678	31.8
AFR	74	75	69	72	2.7
ANG	549	530	423	387	29.5
Total	1617	1537	1184	1137	29.7

SOURCE: Headquarters United States Air Force (AF/A3O-A), "Alt FY15 POM Fighter Impacts and Recommendations," 2013.

Production Versus Absorption

The Air Force has often set fighter pilot training production goals based on sustainment needs. Recall that annual steady-state sustainment is given by the formula

$$Sustainment = \frac{Requirements}{TARS}.$$

This focus, however, ignores the intervening constraint represented by absorption, and sometimes means that fighter production goals present a moving target to aircrew managers.[1]

As described in Chapter Two, overabsorption of inexperienced pilots results in unacceptably slow progression to the experienced threshold and unfavorable readiness conditions. These conditions were notably observed in the A-10 fighter wing at Pope Air Force Base in 2000, giving rise to the term "Pope syndrome" to indicate the impacts of too many inexperienced pilots in a unit. Taylor et al. (2002) demonstrated that these conditions begin to appear when the proportion of experienced pilots in a squadron falls below 60 percent. That study characterized the health of operational fighter units as shown in Table D.2.[2]

---

[1] Dramatic cuts in undergraduate pilot production made during the post–Cold War drawdown created a fighter pilot "bathtub." Total undergraduate pilot production for all MDSs dropped from more than 1,500 AC pilots per year in FYs 1989–1990 to about 500 in FYs 1994–1996. See Taylor et al. (2002) and Taylor, Bigelow, and Ausink (2009) for more information on the creation of, as well as the issues with, the fighter pilot bathtub. Attempting to refill the bathtub by bringing production numbers up to sustainment levels was especially stressful to the system.

[2] The Pope Syndrome conditions are documented in Taylor et al. (2002, pp. 5–14) and revisited in Taylor, Bigelow, and Ausink (2009). See also Appendix D. While the RAND recommendation for a 60 percent experienced level helps maintain a buffer for absorption capability, the Air Force minimum goal of 55 percent set at the 1999 Four-Star Summit has, in order to maximize absorption capacity, effectively become a maximum goal.

Table D.2. Descriptive Terms for Operational Units

Description	Characteristics
Healthy	100% manned
	~60% experienced
	Inexperienced pilots can fly at the sorties per crew per month (SCM) average for combat mission ready (CMR) pilots
Stressed	Units are manned at no more than 110%
	~45% experienced
	Inexperienced pilots struggle to maintain CMR
Broken	~120% manned
	<40% experienced
	New pilots do not become experienced in 36 months

Fighter Pilot Production Anomalies

Production goals to meet sustainment requirements have been established at four-star summits or semiannual Corona conferences, but not necessarily funded in subsequent POM processes or carried into the Planning and Programming Guidance Letter, which set the student throughput that was actually funded each year. As an example, the initial 1996 Four-Star Summit, organized to address fighter pilot shortages, set the AC fighter pilot production goal at 370 per year, but that production level was not funded until FY 1999, nor was it ever achieved. Production goals could also be modified to meet absorption constraints, as they were in 1999 when the Air Force recognized its absorption constraints and reduced the production goal to 330 AC pilots per year. However, as indicated in Table D.3, during the period FY 1999 toFY 2013, Summit/Corona production goals were seldom fully funded and never met, as measured by IFF programming and actual production.[3]

---

[3] The IFF course must be completed by all students entering graduate-level training specific to a fighter MDS. Production from this course thus provides a ready measure of how closely the Air Force met its fighter pilot production goals. Production from FTUs is renegotiated annually during a Programmed Flying Training conference to accommodate unexpected earlier attrition and/or external demands generated by TX-Course (for experienced pilots to regain currency or transition to another fighter) and I-Course (for instructor pilot, or IP, upgrades) demands. As a result, neither ACC, which operates two of the fighter FTUs (A-10s and F-15Es), nor the ANG, which operates two of three F-16 FTUs (Tucson and Kelly) and the only remaining F-15C FTU (Kingsley), maintains a comprehensive database reflecting programmed and actual FTU production numbers. Fortunately, AETC does maintain a comprehensive database for the IFF course.

Table D.3. AC Fighter Pilot Production Goals and Actual Production

Fiscal Year	Summit/Corona Goals (Unfunded)	Programmed IFF Production	Actual IFF Production
1999	370	370	362
2000	330	344	288
2001	330	310	314
2002	330	330	288
2003	330	331	303
2004	324	330	312
2005	308	308	297
2006	308	309	289
2007	330	245	237
2008	330	305	196
2009	297	304	191
2010	224	191	160
2011	224	221	178
2012	243	190	157
2013	243	195	203

NOTES: Funded IFF goals and actual production from AETC/A3R.
Unfunded goals from AF /A3O-A.

The relationship of training production goals and actual production to pilot inventories and requirements is displayed graphically for each of the three components in Figure D.2. The red bars depict actual funded IFF production goals, as shown in the respective Planning and Programming Guidance Letters, while the blue bars show the actual IFF graduates for each fiscal year, both using the right axis. The black line, also using the right axis, depicts (possibly) unfunded production goals that were established during Four-Star Summits, Coronas, etc. The red and blue lines, using the left axis, specify fighter pilot requirements (red line) and inventory (blue line) for the indicated period. Comparison of the three figures indicates that RC inventory shortfalls have been comparable to the magnitude of AC shortfalls, but proportionally greater.

Figure D.2. Fighter Pilot Production Goals, Inventories, and Requirements

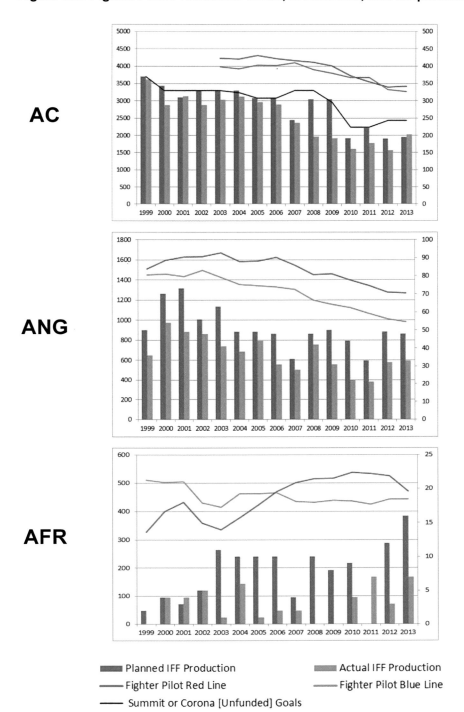

SOURCES: For AC, red line and blue line are from Headquarters United States Air Force (AF/A3O-A), "Alt FY15 POM Fighter Impacts and Recommendations," 2013. For ANG and AFR, red lines are from Air Force requirements files developed by RAND; blue lines are from Air Force inventory files developed by RAND; IFF goals and production, and Summit/Corona goals are from AETC/A3R.
NOTES: Red line (requirements) and blue line (inventory) are plotted on the left axis. IFF planned (red bars) and actual (blue bars) production and Summit/Corona goals (black line) are plotted on the right axis. Summit/Corona goals were not recorded for the ANG and AFRC.

From FY 1999 through FY 2013, the three components missed programmed fighter pilot production numbers, on average, by 12 percent for the AC, 28 percent for the ANG, and 58 percent for AFRC. In the AC, however, the programmed production in many of those years would also have exceeded absorption capacity. The RCs did not face a similar absorption constraint, and thus their training production shortfalls have contributed to possibly avoidable inventory shortfalls.

Ironically, while fighter pilot inventories would have been greater if all production goals had been met, the Air Force would likely have been worse off in other important respects. As noted in Taylor, Bigelow, and Ausink (2009, p. 15), the adverse training conditions that existed at Pope Air Force Base in 2000 "would have been more extensive and would have lasted longer had the production goal of 330 fighter pilots per year [until 2003] been maintained. Thus, the full effects of exceeding a realistic absorption limit were not fully realized at the time." Modeling used during the Transformational Aircrew Management Initiatives for the 21st Century (TAMI-21) initiative in 2006 (Taylor, Bigelow, and Ausink, 2009, p. 61) estimated that to restore units to a healthy status, as defined in Table D.2, only 200 fighter pilots should be produced annually by FY 2016 (see Appendix E). TAMI-21 participants recognized that this level of production would not meet total fighter pilot requirements, and so examined options for alternative approaches to filling them or options that would reduce the number of positions. Figure D.3, which shows how actual IFF production compared to two potential levels of absorption capacity during the last fifteen years, suggests that absorption capacity has declined below the TAMI-21 projection of 200 per year and that production has likely exceeded absorption capacity for much of this period.[4]

---

[4] We have not assembled the data needed to calculate precise absorption capacities during this 15-year period. We note, however, that an annual absorption capacity of 0.22 per PMAI for the AC is consistent with a fighter unit meeting its minimum Ready Aircrew Program requirements.

Figure D.3. AC Fighter Pilot Absorption Capacity and Production

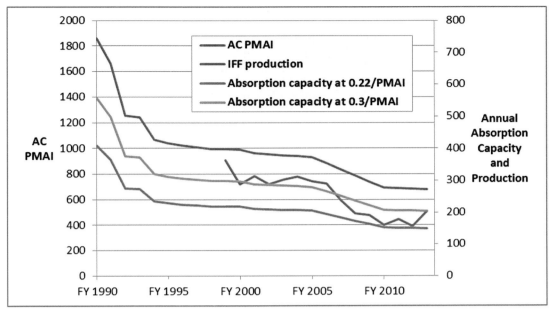

SOURCES: PMAI - Headquarters United States Air Force (AF/A3O-A), "Alt FY15 POM Fighter Impacts and Recommendations," 2013; IFF production – AETC/A3R; absorption capacity – PAF calculations.

Lessons Learned

Our net assessment of fighter pilot dynamics over the past several decades is that the system has been out of balance since the post–Cold War drawdown. A fundamental problem is that, when required sustainment levels exceed absorption capacities and cause production levels to exceed absorption limits, the health of the operational units is degraded. The resulting imbalances, in turn, can generate abrupt corrective actions, such as lowering production levels to reduce stress in these units (see Table D.3). These actions, although essential to prevent stressed or broken units, tend to drive the fighter aircrew management system even further away from the required equilibrium among the production, absorption and sustainment elements. This is because lower production levels inevitably produce lower future inventories, further exacerbating the original pilot shortfall problems. While preventing broken units may clearly take precedence over building larger inventories, these issues illustrate system complexities and the consequences of efforts to operate its elements under sustained saturated[5] (or supersaturated) conditions. They also further illustrate the requirement to bring these elements completely into balance.

---

[5] The production and absorption processes are dynamic queuing systems that become "saturated" when operated consistently at or near 100 percent of capacity. External factors will generate perturbations within the system that require adjustments to restore balance. The ability to make these adjustments requires buffers. Saturated systems are inherently unstable and become very difficult to adjust and return to equilibrium conditions. A 15–20 percent buffer is suggested in the research literature to ensure that essential adjustments can be made (Kleinrock, 1975).

Appendix E: Post–Cold War Aircrew Management Decisions

- 1992 cut in new pilot production
  - Total production lowered from 1,500 AC pilots per year from FY 1989–1990 to 500 per year from FYs 1994–1996
- 1995–2000 "peace dividend" fighter PMAI cuts (see Figure D.1)
  - Cut from 3,170 PMAI in FY 1990 to 1,801 PMAI in FY 1995
  - And eventually to 1,617 PMAI by FY 2000
- 1995 Base Realignment and Closure (BRAC)
  - Saturated undergraduate pilot training by requiring near-100 percent production levels
- 1996 Summit
  - Set pilot production goals at 1,100 (total) and 370 (fighters)
- 1999 Summit
  - Maintained 1,100 total goal, dropped fighters to 330 (with 30 more to be absorbed in ANG/AFRC units) and set experience objective of 55 percent
    - The 30 AC fighter pilots to be absorbed in ARC units initiative was conceptually similar to current 8/80 and 4/40 initiatives, but was never implemented
- 2001 Summit
  - Addressed "Pope syndrome" and other stressed or broken units
  - Confirmed 1100/330 in active units only
  - Reset experience goal to 45 percent minimum to accommodate absorption issues
- 2003 Corona
  - Continued to address "Pope syndrome" conditions in other units
  - One-time 10 percent "throttle back" in total and fighter production goals (implemented incrementally over a single Future Year Defense Program)
- 2005 Aircrew Review
  - Convened to address continuing overmanning and underexperiencing issues in ops units
  - RAND's Dynamic Absorption Model indicated that existing policies would stress or break every absorbing fighter MDS fleet by FY 2010
- 2005 BRAC
  - Closed five F-16 squadrons (three at Cannon, one each at Mt. Home and Eielson)

- Prevented these squadrons from absorbing new pilots during transition period (even though the PAA were eventually redistributed)
- Raised the manning level for the F-16 wing at Misawa, for example, from a manageable 105 percent in September 2006 to 126 percent in January 2007, eventually reaching a distinctly unmanageable 141 percent by May 2007
  - Spread IFF to SUPT bases
    - Also disrupted IFF training, slowing production and creating breaks in training, during the transition period

- 2006 Air Force Smart Operations for the 21st Century (AFSO-21) initiative
  - Proposed substituting MTC simulator sessions for flying hours in RAP requirements and experience definition
  - Only F-15Cs had MTCs in 2006; PAF analysis indicated that continuing to pump new F-15C pilots into operational units at the programmed rates could bring manning levels down from 125+ percent to 105 percent
    - But would cause a second-tour "choke point," preventing essential second-tour pilots from joining the units to fly as IPs and supervisors.
  - Initiated 10 percent flying hour cuts to offset MTC costs, to occur across FY 2008–2013 Future Year Defense Program
    - Flying-hour cuts occurred in all fighter MDSs, despite the fact that only F-15Cs had MTCs at the time

- 2006 Transformational Aircrew Management Initiatives for the 21st Century (TAMI-21) initiative
  - PAF analysis, using its Dynamic Absorption Model, indicated all absorbing fighter units would be broken if programmed production levels were not reduced
  - PAF recommended dropping incrementally to 229 fighter pilots in 2011 and eventually decreasing to 200 fighter pilots in 2014
  - Other recommendations included establishing an RPA career field and using ANG and AFR units to absorb AC pilots[1]
  - CSAF did not accept recommendations, instead returned to 1100 total and 330 fighter pilot production levels and terminated preliminary experiments for an RPA career field

- 2007 Four-Star Conference
  - Agreed to limit flows of new pilots into saturated units, and gave limited authority to AF/A3O to manage production between 950 and 1,050 pilots per year

---

[1] The TAMI-21 recommendations listed here are not to be confused with the TAMI-21 Initiatives that moved SUPT graduates and low-experience fighter and bomber pilots into RPA units and would eventually be publicized by the Air Force in May 2007. See Taylor, Bigelow, and Ausink (2009) for more information.

- 2009 Rated Staff IPT
  - Cut fighter requirements by 224 billets, principally by converting staff and test billets from military to civilian [2]
- 2010 CAF Redux [3]
  - Cut 6 percent of F-16 PMAI and 22 percent of F-16 PTAI
  - Cut 31 percent of F-15 PMAI and 69 percent of F-15C PTAI
  - Cut only ~150 fighter billets, mostly in training and operational units
- 2011 Fighter IPT
  - Prepared for Rated Summit 11
- 2011 Rated Summit
  - Addressed absorption issues by proposing 8/80 active associate units in ARC units
  - Addressed production constraints by
    - Removing training sorties from the F-16 FTU syllabus, Increasing throughput at ANG-managed FTUs (Tucson, Kelly, and Kingsley)
  - Set Total Force production goals at 278 (243 AC and 35 RC)
    - Not currently fully funded
    - If fully funded and met, would exceed current absorption capacity

---

[2] Source: RSAP History 2004-2013v1.xlsx, AF/A3O-AM.

[3] Sources: RSAP History 2004-2013v1.xlsx, AF/A3O-AM & Fighter RL-BL Evolution v4.pptx, 17 Mar 14, AF/A3O-AT

Appendix F: Previous Reductions in Nonabsorbing Fighter Pilot Positions

This appendix provides information on past shortfalls in nonabsorbing positions, how reductions have been taken over the past decade in those positions, and difficulty in assessing the impacts of those reductions.

Past Prioritizations and Reductions

Figure F.1 shows how annual RSAPs over the past decade prioritized the fill of overall pilot and fighter pilot requirements outside of line flying units. This figure illustrates that

- Historically, both overall pilot billets and fighter pilot billets have been undermanned.
- Fighter pilot billets have been more undermanned than the broader set of pilots overall
- The number of fighter pilot billets decreased proportionally more than the number of overall pilots.

Figure F.1. RSAP Prioritizations for Requirements Outside of Line Flying Units (FYs 2004–2014)

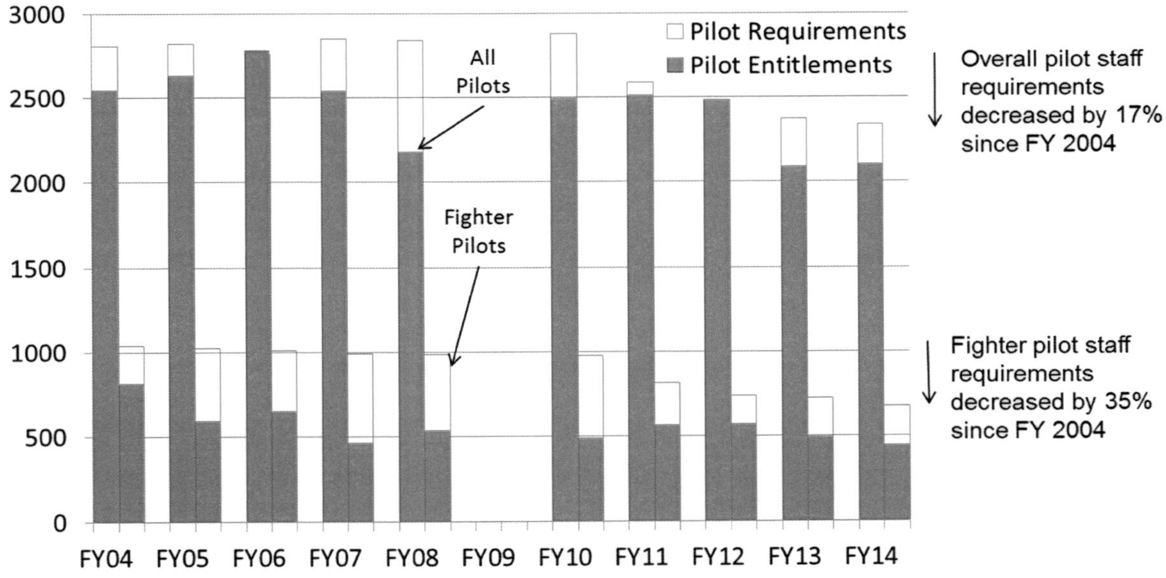

SOURCE: RSAP documents; no published RSAP available for FY 2009.

Figure F.2 shows the changes in fighter pilot billets from FY 2009 to FY 2014 for organizations and activities with more than ten fighter pilots assigned (note that bars to the right of zero represent reductions; those to the left represent increases). Even though the aggregate number of billets decreased by 345 over this period, some units saw an increase; changes to specific staffs reflect policy decisions by the Air Force, Department of Defense, and joint organizations. Reflected in this figure are decisions to limit the number of fighter pilots serving in an ALO role, the elimination of Joint Forces Command, and corporate reviews of and direction to Air Force staffs to reduce manning requirements. Presumably some of the authorizations were formally added to reflect manning that was always present but not formally codified, such as at the Air Force Academy or Air University.

Figure F.2. Change in Fighter Pilot Authorization in Air Liaison Officer, Staff, Joint, and Test Flying Organizations (FYs 2009–2014)

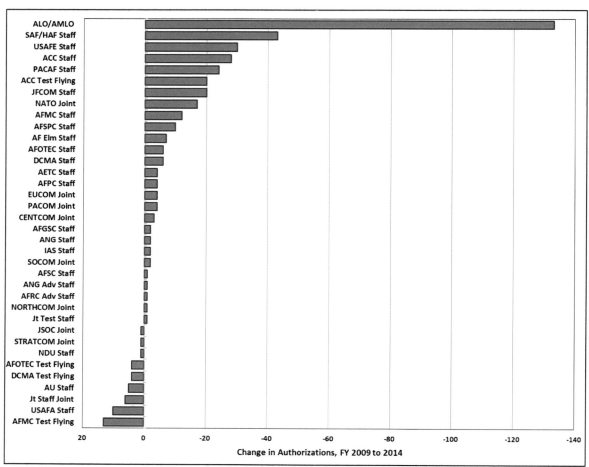

NOTES: SAF = Secretary of the Air Force, HAF = Headquarters Air Force, USAFE = United States Air Forces in Europe, PACAF = Pacific Air Forces, JFCOM = Joint Forces Command, NATO = North Atlantic Treaty Organization, AFMC = Air Force Material Command, AFSPC = Air Force Space Command, AF Elm = Air Force element [of a Defense, joint, or international activity], AFOTEC = Air Force Operational Test and Evaluation Command, DCMA = Defense Contract Management Agency, EUCOM = U.S. European Command, PACOM = U.S. Pacific Command, CENTCOM = U.S. Central Command, AFGSC = Air Force Global Strike Command, ANG = Air National Guard, IAS = Air Force International Affairs, SOCOM = U.S. Special Operations Command, NORTHCOM = U.S. Northern Command, Jt = joint, JSOC = Joint Special Operations Command, STRATCOM = U.S. Strategic Command, NDU = National Defense University, AU = Air University, USAFA = United States Air Force Academy.

Figure F.3 takes a closer look at the authorizations at Air Force staffs over the last decade. All staffs reduced authorizations with the exception of Air University (AU). The four Air Force staffs with the largest number of fighter pilots all significantly reduced requirements over this time period. The staff with the largest requirement and absolute reduction, ACC, reduced its requirement by about a third. The next three largest staffs, Pacific Air Forces (PACAF), Air Force Secretariat and Headquarters (SAF/HAF), and United States Air Forces in Europe (USAFE) each reduced their requirements for fighter pilots by about half over this same period.

Figure F.3. Air Force Staff Fighter Pilot Authorizations, FYs 2004–2014

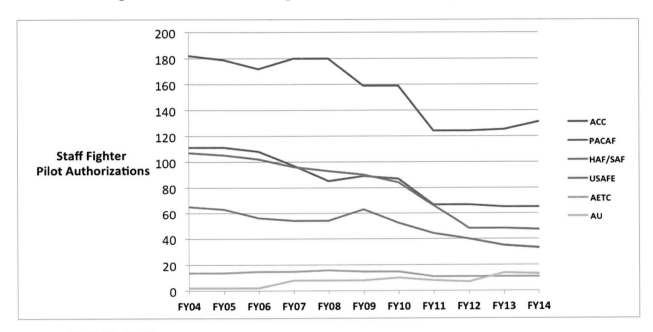

SOURCE: RSAPs.
NOTE: Includes staffs with ten or more authorizions. See note for Figure 4.2 for identification of abbreviations.

Impact of Reductions

To attempt to understand the impact of these reductions and the potential for further reductions, we interviewed staff officers and leaders at ACC, including personnel from the Directorate of Operations (ACC/A3), and the Directorate of Manpower, Personnel, and Services (ACC/A1). Compared with 2004, in 2014 ACC had two-thirds as many fighter pilot authorizations, but only half of these were actually filled with fighter pilots. So ACC's assigned fighter pilots are now about one-third of the authorizations it had ten years ago. Despite the large difference between historical authorizations and the current fill rate of the remaining positions, it is difficult for the command to articulate what work is not accomplished because of unfilled staff positions. There is a sentiment among those we interviewed that most work is getting done, but only superficially. The inability to articulate the impact of reduced manning is exacerbated by a manning planning

61

horizon that is relatively short-term, driven by the assignment cycle process. There is no tracking of chronically unfilled positions. However, there was some awareness among those we interviewed of positions where subject-matter expertise is lacking (e.g., weapon system–specific expertise or weapon school graduates). Without better position tracking over time or other criteria that measure the work done at ACC and other major commands, it is not clear to us whether there are measurable consequences for filling categories at less than 100 percent, or whether it is acceptable to leave them unfilled or filled by non–fighter pilots.

References

AFI—*See* Air Force Instruction.

Air Force Instruction 11-412, *Aircrew Management*, Washington, D.C., December 10, 2009.

Air Force Instruction 38-201, *Management of Manpower Requirements and Authorizations*, Washington, D.C., May 14, 2013.

Anderegg, C. Richard, *Sierra Hotel: Flying Air Force Fighters in the Decade After Vietnam*, Washington, D.C.: Air Force History and Museums Program, 2001.

Department of the Air Force, "Great Deal of Symmetry Between AF, National Commission Recommendations," news release, February 7, 2014. As of July 23, 2015: http://www.af.mil/News/ArticleDisplay/tabid/223/Article/473288/great-deal-of-symmetry-between-af-national-commission-recommendations.aspx

Department of the Air Force, "Air Force Announces Change to Headquarters Organization," news release, July 14, 2014. As of July 23, 2015: http://www.af.mil/News/ArticleDisplay/tabid/223/Article/486175/air-force-announces-changes-to-headquarters-organization.aspx

Headquarters United States Air Force (AF/A1 and AF/A3/5), "Rated Staff Requirements IPT Implementation," memorandum, Washington, D.C.: Department of the Air Force, August 3, 2009.

Headquarters United States Air Force (AF/A3/5 Reserve Advisor), "RSAP Process Improvements," briefing at Aircrew Summit 2014, Washington D.C.: Department of the Air Force, September 18, 2014.

Headquarters United States Air Force (AF/A3O-A), "CAF Active Association (AA) Update and Vector Check," briefing at Aircrew Summit 2014, Washington D.C.: Department of the Air Force, September 18, 2014.

Headquarters United States Air Force (AF/A3O-A), "Alt FY15 POM Fighter Impacts and Recommendations," briefing at Aircrew Summit 2013, Washington D.C.: Department of the Air Force, September 19, 2013.

Headquarters United States Air Force (AF/A3O-A), "Rated Staff Allocation Plan (RSAP)," briefing at Aircrew Management Executive Council meeting, Washington D.C.: Department of the Air Force, October 30, 2013.

Headquarters United States Air Force (AF/A3O-AI), "Rated Summit Requirements Review," briefing at Aircrew Management Executive Council meeting, Washington, D.C.: Department of the Air Force, December 15, 2011.

Headquarters United States Air Force (MA to CSAF), "CSAF Vector Check on ARC Requirements Management Process Improvement Initiative," briefing at Aircrew Summit 2014, Washington D.C.: Department of the Air Force, September 18, 2014.

Kleinrock, Leonard, *Queuing Systems*, Vol. 1, New York: John Wiley & Sons, 1975.

Myers, Daniel, "CS 547 Lecture 12: The M/M/1 Queue," Massachusetts Institute of Technology lecture, undated. As of July 30, 2015: http://pages.cs.wisc.edu/~dsmyers/cs547/lecture_12_mm1_queue.pdf

National Commission on the Structure of the Air Force, *Report to the President and Congress of the United States*, Washington, D.C., January 30, 2014. As of July 23, 2015: http://afcommission.whs.mil/public/docs/NCSAF%20WEB220.pdf

Robbert, Albert A., *Costs of Flying Units in Air Force Active and Reserve Components*, Santa Monica, Calif.: RAND Corporation, TR-1275-AF, 2013. As of July 23, 2015: http://www.rand.org/pubs/technical_reports/TR1275.html

Robbert, Albert A., James H. Bigelow, John E. Boon, Jr., Lisa Harrington, Michael McGee, S. Craig Moore, Daniel M. Norton, and William W. Taylor, *Suitability of Missions for Air Force Reserve Components*, Santa Monica, Calif.: RAND Corporation, RR-429-AF, 2014. As of July 23, 2015: http://www.rand.org/pubs/research_reports/RR429.html

Stallings, William, "Queuing Analysis," undated. As of July 30, 2015: http://www.cosc.brocku.ca/Offerings/3P96/notes/QueuingAnalysis.pdf

Taylor, William W., S. Craig Moore, and Charles Robert Roll, Jr., *The Air Force Pilot Shortage: A Crisis for Operational Units?* Santa Monica, Calif.: RAND Corporation, MR-1204-AF, 2000. As of July 23, 2015: http://www.rand.org/pubs/monograph_reports/MR1204/

Taylor, William W., James H. Bigelow, S. Craig Moore, Leslie Wickman, Brent Thomas, and Richard S. Marken, *Absorbing Air Force Fighter Pilots: Parameters, Problems, and Policy Options*, Santa Monica, Calif.: RAND Corporation, MR-1550-AF, 2002. As of July 23, 2015: http://www.rand.org/pubs/monograph_reports/MR1550/

Taylor, William W., James H. Bigelow, and John A. Ausink, *Fighter Drawdown Dynamics: Effects on Aircrew Inventories*, Santa Monica, Calif.: RAND Corporation, MG-855-AF, 2009. As of July 23, 2015:
http://www.rand.org/pubs/monographs/MG855/

Wikipedia, "M/M/1 Queue," 2014. As of July 30, 2015:
https://en.wikipedia.org/wiki/M/M/1_queue